THE GAY
VACATION GUIDE

THE GAY VACATION GUIDE

The Best Trips and How to Plan Them

REVISED AND UPDATED

MARK CHESNUT

Kensington Publishing Corp.
http://www.kensingtonbooks.com

KENSINGTON BOOKS are published by

Kensington Publishing Corp.
850 Third Avenue
New York, NY 10022

All Kensington titles, imprints and distributed lines are available at special quantity discounts for bulk purchases for sales promotion, premiums, fund raising, educational or institutional use.

Special book excerpts or customized printings can also be created to fit specific needs. For details, write or phone the office of the Kensington Special Sales Manager: Kensington Publishing Corp., 850 Third Avenue, New York, NY, 10022. Attn. Special Sales Department. Phone: 1-800-221-2647.

Kensington and the K logo Reg. U.S. Pat. & TM Off.

ISBN 0-7582-0266-0

First Citadel Press Printing: 1997
First Kensington Trade Paperback Printing: November 2002

10 9 8 7 6 5 4 3 2 1

Printed in the United States of America

This book is dedicated to my mother, Eunice Clayton Chesnut, who gave me the travel bug and always made sure I had a typewriter; and to my sister, Glynn, who patiently listened to my whining as I wrote this book.

Thanks also to Marybeth Anastasio, J.J. Catanzarita, Claudette Covey, Mark "Gunther" Porter, Lisa Reilly Cullen, Rob Stein, Rich Volo, and Laura Wise for their friendship and support, as well as all the other people who were interviewed for this book.

I also must express my great appreciation for the faith that David Andrusia and Katharine Sands showed in my work, which made this book possible.

Most of all, this book is dedicated to my partner in love and travel, Angel Pabón. Not only has he stayed with me through all the high-maintenance moments of my adult life, he also served as a researcher for this book.

CONTENTS

INTRODUCTION

> "Passage, immediate passage!
> The blood burns in my veins!
> . . . Have we not stood here like trees
> in the ground long enough?"
>
> —Walt Whitman

When I was growing up, the event I looked forward to more than anything else was going to visit my grandparents in Kentucky. Especially at Christmas, when the threat of blizzards made driving too risky, and we had to board a glamorous Allegheny Airlines DC-9 to make the trip. Sitting back in a plush, shocking-orange seat (coach, of course), I felt like I had the world at my fingertips. I was excited beyond belief.

Maybe it was because I was anxious to get away from a not-always-pleasant school life. Maybe it was because I knew that my grandparents—and some Christmas presents—were waiting somewhere at the end of my trip. (It may have also been because I had overdosed on the movie *Airport,* suffered from a flight attendant fetish, and enjoyed getting high from aviation fuel.)

One thing was certain: I was addicted to travel. Whether it was by plane, car, or bus, I wanted to travel, I wanted to get away, I wanted to see the world—even if for me the world was limited to Rochester, New York, Louisville, and Paducah, Kentucky.

The difference is that now, as an adult, I have more control over my destiny and my destinations. But I still suffer from a severe case of wanderlust. You probably do, too. It's not an uncommon affliction among gay men and women. Indeed, one of the few common threads that bind our diverse community together is that we love to travel. Even when we can't afford other things, we set aside money to get away. Whatever it is we're looking for—adventure, escape, camaraderie, romance, sex, relaxation, or just plain acceptance—we seem to find it on the road.

So what do you look for when *you* travel? And what are you doing on *your* next vacation? If you need some ideas, read on. . . .

There are more options right now for gay travelers than you could probably imagine. You could take a gay square dancing tour of Australia, a gay cruise up the Nile, or swim with dolphins—as well as a bunch of gay people—in the Bahamas. All kinds of companies, from airlines to tour operators to hotels, are clamoring for your business. The choices are so overwhelming, how can you possibly sort through all the options and figure out what's right for you?

That's where this book comes into play. It is, as far as I know, the first true guide to gay and lesbian vacations. I emphasize the word *vacations,* because there are already plenty of destination guides out there. Rather than focusing on *destinations,* we're going to take a look at the many *categories* of travel now open to gay men and lesbians. So if you have a hankering for horseback riding or an aching for an all-inclusive resort, you'll know where to look. You won't have to wade through pages of city listings to find general information about travel, activities, or tours, and you won't have to wait for articles to appear in travel magazines or newspapers.

Nearly all of the types of travel listed in this book have been offered in a mainstream format for a long time. After all, there's nothing new about horseback riding, hiking, cruising, or visiting a resort. And gay people have certainly enjoyed themselves in many mainstream settings. So why this sudden explosion in gay travel options?

One of the main reasons, of course, is money. Travel-related companies are now starting to realize just how much spending power our community wields, and they want a piece of it. In addition, more gay and lesbian entrepreneurs are starting up their own businesses. In short, more and more businesses are reaping the rewards of serving our needs.

It's a wide range of needs, as illustrated throughout this book. There is no single set of interests and concerns that applies to every lesbian and gay traveler. Still, we share a few common concerns when it comes to vacation time (and these concerns also set us apart from our straight counterparts):

- Gay and lesbian travelers need to feel safe and comfortable in their vacation environment—which is not possible in every mainstream setting.
- We often have to hide our sexual orientation during our workaday lives, and usually want to be open and relaxed during vacations, without fear of discrimination.
- We sometimes like the opportunity to interact socially, sexually, or romantically with other people like us.

Sure, there are other traits common to some gay and lesbian travelers. Gay men, for example, may be more likely to want a sexually-charged atmosphere during their vacation (this doesn't have so much to do with the fact that we're gay as it does with the fact that all men are pigs, according to some theories). My friend Veronica pointed out that lesbians stereotypically would be more interested in camping than straight people. Whether that's true or not, I'll leave to the statisticians.

The point is, we *are* different, and while we can have a wonderful time during a straight vacation, sometimes nothing less than a gay vacation will do.

"It's about freedom," explains Ken, a New Yorker who first took an all-gay vacation in the late eighties. Ken's visit to a gay resort marked the first time he felt safe holding his lover's hand in public. "Up until that point, I never really felt comfortable.

Visiting that gay resort really helped me relax, and it even changed how I felt about myself as a gay person."

The Growing Gay and Lesbian Market

Back in the early 1970s, when Hanns Ebensten first began arranging tour groups for gay men, Pan American World Airways repeatedly refused to carry them. Gay tours just weren't done, at least not openly on a major airline. But this didn't stop Ebensten from seeing the potential. He formed Hanns Ebensten Travel, a pioneer in the gay travel market.

Ebensten's initial offerings included a trip down the Colorado River. "Now, twenty years since I started these trips," the Key West–based businessman writes in his book, *Volleyball With the Cuna Indians*, "there is no longer any novelty, oddity, or surprise in seeing gay [people] on the Colorado River each summer."

Or flying on major airlines, for that matter. Indeed, two of the surest indicators of the booming market for lesbian and gay travel are the growing acceptance of the gay market by mainstream companies, and the increasing number of air and land packages made especially for us.

Even in the few short years since the first edition of this book was published, the increased attention on the gay and lesbian market has been incredible. Today, every major airline has made at least some effort to show their fondness for us—and hotel companies and tour operators have scrambled to let us know they want our business.

The companies that address our needs are the ones that have an edge when it comes to maintaining profitability. That's because gay people travel a lot and are a highly desirable, more affluent market. We are also loyal to companies that meet our needs, and refer these companies to our friends.

According to a recent survey by Community Marketing, Inc., a company that specializes in the gay travel market, 54 percent of American lesbians and gays took international vacations within the past twelve months (vs. a national average of nine percent). Compared to our straight friends, we're practically always on the road. And according to a survey by Plog Research reported in Travel Weekly, gays and lesbians spend more money on leisure travel (a mean of $3,059 in a 12-month period for gay travelers, vs. $2,529 for all respondents).

We gay people are increasingly taking gay-specific, prepackaged trips, which is evident in the amount of space in this book dedicated to air and land packages. The number of gay tour operators and travel businesses has grown by leaps and bounds in recent years, producing hundreds of new companies and thousands of new travel opportunities.

The advantage of package deals is that they frequently—but not always—provide more travel or better amenities for less money than if you'd arranged the package on your own.

Whether gay or straight, package deals generally fall into one of two categories: those that don't have an escort and those that do. The price of a simple unescorted package deal usually includes accommodations and perhaps air and some meals or other extras, but offer no guide to lead you and no set itinerary once you reach your destination. You're free to explore and relax on your own.

Escorted tours, on the other hand, provide a guide who will lead you throughout the trip. The guide's services are included in the price you pay, and there is usually an extensive itinerary.

With escorted tours, you don't have to worry about every little detail of your trip; you can sit back, relax, and take in the sites while the tour guide makes sure that everything goes smoothly. Group tours are also highly conducive to socializing and making new acquaintances.

Escorted group tours usually include some travel by air, ship, and/or motorcoach. Package prices may include some meals or all of them; admission to various attractions during the trip; and fees related to other activities.

As much as some people love group tours, they are not for everyone. Escorted travel allows for limited flexibility: You must choose one of the existing dates scheduled for the trip, and once you're there, most of the activities are predetermined.

You're also going to see the same group of people throughout the vacation. I wouldn't exactly call this the most creative or stimulating way to travel.

Another warning: Don't automatically assume that group travel or packages will save you money. One of the problems traditionally associated with gay travel products is that they sometimes cost more than equivalent mainstream programs. This is changing as the market expands and matures, but shop around to find something that best fits your budget.

Deciding on a tour is an individual process. It may depend on the destination you want to visit. Are there numerous tours offered? Is it a place you'd feel comfortable visiting by making your own plans? Based on airfare and the type of accommodation you desire, what is the average cost of visiting the place on your own versus the cost of a group tour? (If you're willing to stay in real budget accommodations and not eat extravagantly, you can often beat the price of a tour.)

Independent travel allows travelers to more closely control the modes of transport and the class of accommodations— thereby keeping a tighter reign on expenses. If money is a concern, for example, rail and bus passes available in several countries can help to cut the cost of ground transportation, while hostels can sharply reduce the cost of accommodations if you can do without glamour. And, even with all the attention we're paying to gay-specific packages, don't forget that you may belong to other categories of travelers that are eligible for discounts, such as senior citizens or students.

People who like the idea of a package deal but want the flexibility of independent travel usually end up buying a hotel/air package—the kind common for destinations like Las Vegas, Florida, and the Caribbean—where there is no planned itinerary. With these packages, it doesn't matter much whether it's from a gay or a mainstream company, as long as you know where you're going. But there are an increasing number of gay-specific packages to note.

Being curious and well-informed pays off in the long run. Whether you're planning to join a gay group tour, or simply making hotel reservations for a quick weekend getaway, make sure you know what you're getting into. Don't believe every- thing the brochures say; ask questions of your travel agent, the person at the other end of the phone, or even friends who've already taken the trip. If you don't understand the terms used in describing a resort or a tour package, ask. If the brochure promises "breakfast daily" as part of the price, is it a full, sit- down American breakfast or a "raid-the-refrigerator" self-serve meal?

Also check on cancellation policies ahead of time—will you get a refund or credit if you need to cancel? What if the trip is cancelled by the tour operator?

* * *

All these questions, just for a little escape! Times sure have changed since the days when we were strapped into shocking- orange airline seats by our mothers. But don't worry—these sundry details shouldn't scare you away from planning your next vacation. The fact is, you *can* painlessly plan a great vacation, and this book will help you do it. So open up your imagination, get out your world map, and fasten your seat belt—you're going on a trip!

HOW TO USE THIS BOOK

The Gay Vacation Guide is arranged to help you to find the information you need about the kind of gay and lesbian travel that interests you most.

This book can be used in several ways: as a source of information when planning a specific vacation, as a general reference guide, or simply as a pleasant getaway for the armchair traveler.

To help you find exactly what you need, the book is divided into several broad categories, such as "Active Vacations" and "Independent Travel." This will help you classify your general travel mood. Within each category, multiple sections focus on specific travel experiences, complete with firsthand impressions, to give you a better feel for the trips.

Of course, no two travelers are looking for the same experience, so I've included entries called "Things to Think About First," which encourage you to decide on trips based on your own personal travel tastes and needs. The "Questions to Ask the Travel Provider" entries can help guide you when speaking with a travel agent or sales rep about a trip, so you'll be sure to get what you want when it's time to make reservations.

The "Travel Tips" sections, which appear throughout the book, offer practical advice—from renting a car to finding lesbian and gay travel services online. Consult the Index or Table of Contents to locate what you need.

The "Resource" entry in each chapter lists companies that offer the kind of travel experiences featured in the section. Remember that there are probably other products and services that these companies offer, and there are probably other companies offering similar travel experiences.

That's where the "Resource Directory," found at the back of this book, comes into play. In it, you'll find a comprehensive list of every tour operator, cruise operator, and travel-related company mentioned in this book, along with a summary of *all* the types of travel products they offer, and full information about how to contact them.

Finally, if you're looking for information about a specific company, destination, or type of travel, you may want to check the "Index" at the very end of the *Guide*, which can pinpoint more of the facts you need to know.

A Few Definitions

To help you get the most from this book, you'll need to understand a few of the terms used throughout the guide. For example, you'll find that most of the travel ideas fall into one of three categories. They are:

GAY AND LESBIAN ONLY   These tour operators and businesses market only to gays and lesbians, and the tour groups are made up of homosexuals (although sensitive straight people may sometimes join in). The advantage is, obviously, the greater sense of comfort that accompanies an all-gay setting.

GAY AND LESBIAN IN A MAINSTREAM SETTING   Some gay tour operators buy blocks of space in mainstream groups—often on cruise ships or large tours—and sell it to gay people. For many kinds of vacations, this works just fine. For instance, the features of an African safari, whether gay or mainstream, probably won't vary much. It's possible to be perfectly comfortable in a mainstream group, and the number of package deals available in the mainstream market may make prices more competitive. The advantage of using a mainstream company listed in this book is that it's more likely to be gay-friendly than a randomly selected company from a newspaper ad.

MEN ONLY AND WOMEN ONLY   Some packages are restricted by gender. This concept has raised some interesting discussions of late. "In many ways, the existence of single-gender travel venues is as insupportable as exclusively heterosexual ones," writes Billy Kolber, editor of *Out & About*, an excellent gay travel newsletter. "How could we denounce Sandals [a Caribbean resort chain] for not allowing gay people at their resorts, and applaud the Royal Palms, which didn't allow women?"

This sort of reasoning has caught on, to some extent. RSVP Travel Productions, which has specialized in all-female and all-male cruises, began offering gay-and-lesbian mixed cruises in 1996. "We will focus on community; all of us all the time," explained Charlie Rounds, RSVP's president.

Still, others say that gender segregation fosters a sense of comfort and community, which they say is justification enough for keeping things separate, at least sometimes. You can assume that the gay travel ideas described in this book are open to both men and women, unless noted otherwise.

While gay travelers enjoy many of the same kinds of travel as anyone else, in this book we'll focus mostly on travel that has a gay element. So-called mainstream travel has already been well catalogued in mainstream travel books.

Accommodations

The Gay Vacation Guide focuses on *categories* of travel—it doesn't attempt to take the place of the many excellent destination guides out there—so you won't find too many listings for accommodations. But in a few cases, when specific destinations are mentioned (as in the section Classic Gay Destinations), you'll find a list of the most highly recommended accommodations for that region, along with detailed information about what each property has to offer and how much a night's stay costs.

The term "full amenities" often appears in the property listings. I use this term to avoid repeating the same information over and over, and perhaps keep you from falling asleep too quickly as you read. For the purposes of this book, a room with full amenities has a telephone, private bathroom with shower and/or tub, daily maid service, and television (cable is now the norm at most properties). Some properties listed are quite comfortable but basic, and don't feature all these amenities; others offer much more, and they are noted with details.

Keep this in mind as you're figuring out your travel plans. Many people who plan on spending all their time outdoors don't care whether or not they have a TV or phone; others, however, want the very best when on vacation, and look for as many amenities as possible. Sometimes, extra features can actually save you money—renting a room with a kitchenette, for example, can allow you to prepare your own meals rather than pay for overpriced restaurant food. The choice is yours, so understanding your own needs, and what various properties have to offer, ensures your satisfaction.

Also listed with each property is the price range. Often, hotels, guesthouses, and resorts offer different rates during their in-season and off-season. Logically enough, in-season (or peak) rates are in effect when the weather is best and the most people are traveling, so prices are accordingly higher. The off-season rates are lower and are better bargains if you're willing to travel during less popular periods of time.

This book lists ranges for peak rates first, followed by the off-season prices. If I've listed only one range of prices, that means it is the year-round range.

What Kind of Travel Should You Look For?

The type of vacation that's right for you depends on your personal preference, and perhaps the activity or package itself. Some things to consider: How comfy are you around straight people? How about homosexuals of the opposite sex? How cuddly do you want to be in public?

Another defining factor that can affect your travel plans is whether you're traveling single, as a couple, or with a group of friends. Most travelers prefer the company of others when vacationing (even so, a wise friend of mine points out that the key to an enjoyable trip is planning to spend as much time *without* your traveling companion as *with*).

Traveling solo can also be immensely rewarding, as you'll probably have interactions and experiences that you wouldn't ordinarily have when traveling with someone. People travel alone for different reasons. Some are looking for companionship and friendship; others relish the time spent just being alone, with limited social interaction.

The downside of traveling alone is that tour operators and hoteliers often charge a "single supplement," an annoying fee that makes it more expensive, on a per-person basis, for one person to travel than two. Ask for suggestions about how this can be avoided—many tour operators, for example, can pair you up with a roommate in order to cut costs.

Whether you're traveling single or as part of a couple, you'll find plenty of travel ideas in this book. Perhaps to a greater extent than the mainstream market, gay and lesbian travel is well prepared to offer exciting travel experiences to both types of travelers. Most gay and lesbian vacation packages are open to singles and couples, although some types of travel better lend themselves to one kind or another. Adventure travel, for example, frequently breeds a sense of camaraderie that makes it easier to befriend other people in a travel group.

If you have a preference one way or another, ask your travel agent or tour operator for suggestions. The more you can tell them about the kind of vacation you're looking for, the more likely you'll be satisfied with your vacation.

The Disclaimer

If you've read any other travel books—gay or not—then you'll understand perfectly what I'm about to say. I've made every effort to ensure that the information presented in this book is current and accurate as of the time of this printing, but as with everything else in life, things change. Businesses open and close; tour packages get cancelled. Prices, of course, are constantly fluctuating in response to market demand. This is why I haven't included specific price information for the tour operators listed here, because by the time you read this book, the package either may no longer be available, or the price may be completely different. At any rate, neither I nor the publisher of this book can be held responsible for any information presented here that is no longer current by the time you read it.

So how do you prevent messing up your travel plans? For one, you should always phone a tour operator, resort, or bar well in advance, or check their Web site for the latest information.

Without a doubt, the absolute best way to make sure your vacation goes smoothly is to consult your friendly travel agent (we'll talk about how to find one in a Travel Tip section). He or she can provide updated information, as well as offer personal expertise that can help guarantee a successful trip.

It's not easy putting together a gay vacation guide. No matter what you do, no matter how much information you have about what you think are the coolest vacations possible, there's going to be something you left out—an experience that someone else found completely wonderful and unforgettable, something that they don't think any other gay traveler should miss.

I've made every effort to include a wide cross section of vacation possibilities, so that whether you're a man or woman, young or old, a beach bunny or history buff, you'll find several ideas here, as well as valuable reference information.

But if there's a particular tip or trip I've left out—or something that you think I *shouldn't* have included—please write and tell me about it. Contact me in care of Kensington Publishing or e-mail me at ChesnutAir@aol.com.

In the meantime, happy traveling.

THE GAY VACATION GUIDE

1

ACTIVE VACATIONS

"I never travel without my diary. One should always have something sensational to read in the train."

—Oscar Wilde

Is it humanly possible? Can you go away for a vacation and come back in better shape than when you left?

That's what happened to Rick. "I was accustomed to going on vacation and eating more, exercising less," he recalls. "So my bicycling trip was kind of different. It was great, actually, because I felt better physically, and it was a lot of fun."

Bicycling is but one of many options for active vacationers. Is rock climbing up a sheer cliff your idea of fun? How about shooting Colorado's rapids in a bright yellow raft? Or a slow, pleasant hike through a national park? If you like to keep moving, then an active vacation could satisfy your needs.

The benefits are multifold. Rather than passively taking in the sights, you participate in activities that let you enjoy all that nature has to offer. You may come back with a richer experience (and maybe even a better body) as a result.

"When people talk about active vacations, they start thinking about adventurous kinds of activities that they may consider too dangerous, like rock climbing," says Rick. "But the truth is, it's not dangerous as long as you're careful and don't take on anything that you can't handle." Indeed, there may be some danger inherent in the trip's activities, but they are generally safe for travelers who take the proper precautions and follow the advice of experienced guides.

"I always thought you had to be some big athlete to take a vacation like this," adds Rick. "But that's not true either." Granted, these vacations aren't for everyone. You should be in relatively good shape and certainly not the couch-potato type. But travelers vary in terms of their physical prowess and experience, and so do vacations. You should ask about the level of difficulty as you shop around. Chicago-based **Toto Tours** rates its adventure tours "easy" to "moderate," which, according to company officials, "means that the average 'Joe' can do them without fear of wreaking havoc to life, limb, or self-esteem. A few have 'high-energy' components which may require doing some physical training in advance, but many of those components are 'optional'—meaning tour participants aren't required to do them if they want to join the tour and enjoy the destination."

An interesting note: People who've taken active vacations usually end up talking as much about the friends they've made as the activities they've done. Active vacations tend to breed friendship and camaraderie to a greater extent than other types of travel, probably because of the intense experiences that the small groups share. That's one reason why active vacations are highly recommended for people traveling alone—you're sure to make new friends. Even if you're traveling with a friend or lover, you're bound to meet people and enjoy sharing experiences.

The closeness fostered by these trips is also why many gays and lesbians prefer to travel with people like themselves, rather than with a mainstream tour. The comfort level is usually greater on a gay and lesbian trip, where no one has to worry about a fellow traveler's reaction to their homosexuality. This sense of comfort and acceptance takes on even greater importance when you're scaling up the side of a mountain and relying on someone to be your buddy.

Comfort levels vary in terms of accommodations, as well. To a greater extent than other tours, lodging for active vacations runs the gamut from five-star luxury hotels to tents in the wilderness. Either can be fine, as long as you get what you want.

THINGS TO THINK ABOUT FIRST   What sports and outdoor activities do you enjoy? What kind of physical shape are you in, and is there an appropriate tour package available for people like you?

QUESTIONS TO ASK THE TRAVEL PROVIDER   How much experience do the tour guides have? Are references available? What levels of skill are required for the tours? What kinds of accommodations are featured? What safety precautions can you offer?

Deals on Wheels: Bicycling Through France

Imagine the wind in your hair, the sun on your back, and your feet on the pedals. For avid cyclists, there's no better way to see the world than by cycling across it. Even for people who don't own a bicycle, it can be a scenic—and healthy—way to travel.

On a seven-day vacation in Provence, Deborah Long bicycled twenty-five to thirty-five miles a day through some of the most beautiful scenery in southern France. "It was really a wonderful way to see that part of France," Deborah says. "It was a lovely trip and a lovely place to go—with a fun group of people."

Deborah and her partner, who hail from Lincoln, Nebraska, toured with **Alyson Adventures,** a company that specializes in active vacations in Europe, the U.S., the South Pacific, and southeast Asia. The company was founded by Sasha Alyson, one of the pioneers in the world of gay publishing, who has since moved into the travel field.

For their bicycle adventure, Deborah rented a 21-speed bicycle from Alyson, although you can opt to bring your own.

Alyson's groups tend to be fairly small—Deborah's was about twelve people. Their trip involved cycling and sightseeing during the day, with evenings spent at various "comfortable" lodgings. Like many active tour providers, Alyson puts out a brochure that explains the difficulty level of each trip. "There were some hills that were a little challenging," Deborah admits. "But you don't have to be a marathon cyclist." If you're planning this kind of trip, ask about the types of terrain that the tour covers, and make sure it sounds right for your level of expertise.

Other trip itineraries include "Big Loire, Little Loire," which features rides through the narrow Renaissance streets in Vendôme and quaint villages in the countryside, en route to several chateaus in central France.

Alyson trips are open to gay men, lesbians, and their friends, although some special excursions are arranged only for single men or women.

Several other companies offer bicycle tours, including **Progressive Travels,** a mainstream tour operator that also offers gay bike tours of France, Italy, and the United States.

Venture Out, based in San Francisco, offers a summertime "Cycling Through Holland" itinerary that features easy cycling through the relatively flat countryside of the Netherlands, visiting towns like Edam, Haarlem, Leiden, Gouda, and Utrecht. The tour wraps up in Amsterdam, just in time for an optional extension to join the city's annual gay pride celebration.

Adventures in Good Company, a Minnesota-based company founded by a former guide from the now-defunct Woodswomen, offers a variety of women-only active itineraries, including a trip called "Cowgirls Don't Get The Blues," which features mountain biking and other outdoor activities at Homestead Ranch, a woman-owned and -operated cattle ranch in Kansas. The company even offers financial assistance programs for single moms.

Idaho-based **WomanTours** also specializes in women-only bike tours. The company has a wide variety of itineraries, including visits to several states in the eastern and western U.S. plus the Canadian Rockies, Hawaii, France, and even Vietnam and New Zealand. Their staff ranges in age from 41 to 62, proving that it's never too late (or too early) to consider taking a biking vacation.

Accommodations vary from tour to tour, but generally are adequately comfortable, although they may not have full amenities such as a phone or TV. But that's not what most cycling vacationers care about, anyway. "It's like a dream come true for me," says Clayton, who recently cycled through France with his lover. "I'd been bicycling around my town for years. But doing it in a foreign country—now *that's* cycling!"

Resources

Adventures in Good Company, 877-439-4042 or 651-998-0120, www.goodaventure.com
Alyson Adventures, 800-825-9766 or 617-542-1177
Progressive Travels, 800-245-2229
Toto Tours, 800-565-1241 or 773-274-8686
Womantours, 800-247-1444

Riding the Rails, Seeing the Sights

Rail vacations don't quite fit into any convenient category. But since the excursions mentioned here involve some hiking and other outdoor activities, I've thrown it in with active vacations.

If rail excursions are to be considered active, then they are a fine example of the "no experience necessary" end of the category. You can enjoy the great outdoors, get some exercise, and not pull every muscle in your body.

Just ask Don Faust, a seventy-one-year-old man who took **Out-West Adventures'** "Montana by Rail" tour, an excursion that also includes some light hiking through the American west in a refurbished classic rail car. With Yellowstone and Glacier National Parks on the itinerary, it was difficult not to see a natural wonder every time he looked out the window.

"It was just one sight-seeing orgy after another," says Don, speaking in the nonbiblical sense, of course. He spent his days in the dome coach, which offers a panoramic view of the scenery. Evenings were spent in hotels and motels along the way, topped off by a visit to the Lazy EL Ranch, a private property owned by the family of OutWest's president, Aaron Kampfe.

Because the tour focused on natural sights, Don notes that it's the kind of tour anyone can go on; you can even bring your grandparents, which is exactly what the tour operator did on that particular trip. "It's good for any person that likes scenery," he explains. "We went through flat country, we saw rams on the side of a mountain, we went through parts where the bald eagle was sitting on the side of a river, and through different mountain ranges. I like plants, I love animals, and I'd never been in that kind of country. I'd been to Pike's Peak in Colorado, but that ain't *nothing* compared to Montana."

Other than a little vertigo at the high altitudes, Don had no problem with the hiking. It was just as enjoyable for him, Don says, as for someone thirty years younger.

Toto Tours offers a gay version of one of North America's most famous rail journeys. Its men-only "Treasures of the Sierra Madre" package crosses bridges and digs into mountain tunnels along Mexico's Copper Canyon route. The eight-night trip departs from Chihuahua, and includes hiking, train rides, cultural exploration, and horseback riding. Group members see high desert lands, mountains and historic villages along the route. Accommodations are in a variety of small hotels along the way, including the Posada Mirador, which sits on the edge of one of the canyon's spectacular viewpoints.

Resources

OutWest Global Adventures, 800-743-0458 or 406-446-1533, www.outwestadventures.com

Toto Tours, 800-565-1241 or 773-274-8686, www.tototours.com

The Undersea World of Gay Divers

Picture this: You've paid a thousand dollars for an exotic, "mainstream" diving vacation, where you'll be viewing some of the most beautiful coral reefs in the world. You're on the boat, getting geared up along with everyone else, as the group leader assigns everyone a "buddy" who will be their partner for the dive—someone to look out for them and help out in case something happens. The leader finally gets to your name—and pairs you up with the one guy on the trip who is so homophobic he'd probably just let you drown if you hit your head on a piece of coral.

Now you're starting to understand why gay dive trips are getting so popular. The camaraderie and interdependence fostered by group dives is a big reason why gay-led trips can be more fun and less stressful. "To be honest, you can get a lot of rednecks on some diving trips," warns Esmond Harmsworth, a Boston-based dive enthusiast who prefers the openness of gay dive trips. He said that mainstream trips sometimes attract an overly macho "Navy Seal" kind of clientele that can be less than gay-friendly. "Even without that risk, they often tend to be boring kinds of people," Esmond adds.

So what's a gay scuba trip like? "I would say the entire thing is a combination of *Waterworld* and *All About Eve*," Esmond quips. This must be a winning combination, because he's already been on six trips with **Undersea Expeditions,** a California-based company established in 1991 that has offered dive trips to Tahiti, Belize, New Guinea, Micronesia, the Caribbean, and Latin America.

Scuba diving and snorkeling open up a colorful world that you really can't imagine until you see it for yourself. Many people begin their love affair with the sea by snorkeling—it's extremely easy and the equipment (flippers, mask, and snorkel) is cheap to rent or buy. Once you're geared up, you just float along and enjoy the sights below. You don't even have to hold your breath or leave the surface of the water if you don't want to. It's an activity that's ideal for many age groups and even someone as unathletic as me can do it.

Diving is more advanced; you must be certified and have access to the more extensive equipment necessary for entering the fascinating world several hundred feet below the sea. Many trips offer certification programs; otherwise you must arrange for instruction and certification before you go (look in the phone book under "scuba" or "diving"). But don't be intimidated by the certification process. Even this activity is enjoyable for travelers with a wide range of abilities.

Accommodations and schedules vary. A recent Belize trip with Undersea Expeditions offered wall diving and accommodations aboard a twenty-passenger luxury ship, where each cabin had a private bath and shower. Also included were three meals daily and complimentary alcoholic and nonalcoholic beverages. A recent trip to Tahiti included seven nights at the Bali Hai Resort, and daily breakfasts.

In addition to specific underwater packages, scuba diving and snorkeling are often available at gay resorts—check the section titled "The Resort Experience" to get more information.

THINGS TO CONSIDER   Are you a certified diver? If not, is certification available during the trip, or will you be certified before? How much time in the water do you want to spend? Do you prefer a live-aboard boat or hotel accommodations?

QUESTIONS TO ASK THE TRAVEL PROVIDER   How many dives—and what other activities and meals—are included in the trip? What kind of accommodations are included—hotel or ship? What is the background of the leader and will any instruction be available? What are some of the diving highlights of the area visited?

Resources

Undersea Expeditions, 800-669-0310 or 858-270-2900, www. underseax.com

Skiing the Gay Slopes

"I don't really like tours," says Steve of Philadelphia. "I don't gravitate toward that kind of thing." But a recent group ski trip, with **OutWest Global Adventures,** helped him to appreciate some of the advantages of going in a group.

"The skiing was really good, but what I liked about it was that it was a tour, but very intimate. We were a small group and it was very personal. For example, the first few nights we stayed in Red Lodge, in a wonderful renovated house that was really beautiful. It wasn't like being in a hotel. The whole trip, you had the feeling that everything was carefully picked."

Because the little details were taken care of, Steve explains, everyone was able to relax faster than on independent ski trips he'd taken. "There was nothing that you had to worry about," he adds. "There were so many things that they paid attention to."

Steve's trip included five days of skiing in Montana, with visits to Red Lodge Mountain's 9,416-foot summit and the 11,150-foot Big Sky Montana. "The terrain varied tremendously," Steve remembers. "Red Lodge was really deep powder skiing. Big Sky was more like a big Western resort." Lift tickets, as well as accommodations and most meals, were included in the package price.

Like many active vacationers, Steve said the camaraderie was a big plus. "One of the things that I liked was that even though the group was small, we came from incredibly diverse backgrounds. So one of the best things was just making new friends. I'm not sure this is for everyone—it wasn't the heavy party disco scene. You'd end up sitting around a fireplace, talking. And the food was fantastic."

Obviously, Steve enjoyed himself. "I would recommend it to anyone from their twenties to their seventies. I think it's probably meant for someone who really likes the outdoors and is interested in getting to know the West better. This is seeing the West with people who know it well. To ski three very different mountains, I think, is terrific. And even though there's no discos with flashing lights, there's a chance to hit bars a couple nights."

OutWest also offers a gay ski tour to Zermatt, Switzerland, high in the Swiss Alps. Visitors stay in a quaint village where no cars are allowed, and enjoy four-star accommodations and dinners.

Additional options come from **Alternative Holidays**, a British tour operator that organizes all-inclusive, gay events at Club Med resorts in both winter and summer. The winter event takes place at a different Alpine Club Med hotel every year. The package includes accommodations, ski pass, ski tuition, all meals and entrance to all evening parties.

For a real sense of togetherness on the slopes (whether you go with a group or not), pay a visit to Aspen, Colorado, for the annual **Aspen Gay Ski Week.** For a whole week, visitors somehow manage to fit skiing into a crowded schedule of parties, benefits, costume competitions, comedy nights, fashion shows, a film festival, and auctions. Among the tour operators offering packages are **OutWest Global Adventures**, which has a record for winning the "downhill costume contest," and **Aspen Ski Tours**, a mainstream ski wholesaler that supports the Aspen Gay & Lesbian Community Fund.

Another similar event is **Lake Tahoe Winterfest,** an annual ski week hosted by the Nevada Gay and Lesbian Visitor & Convention Bureau. The event, which usually takes place in March, includes several entertainment events and parties, and packages are available that include accommodations and some meals.

In February, gay and lesbian ski enthusiasts go north of the border to Whistler, British Columbia, **Altitude**, for the annual **Gay & Lesbian Ski Week at Whistler Resort,** which features dozens of events and activities including picnics, snowmobiling, a barbecue, a mountaintop tea dance, a pool party—and oh, yeah, skiing. OutWest Global Adventures is among the companies offering vacation packages for this event.

For major events, one gay ski enthusiast recommends that "the best thing is to hook up with one of the gay ski clubs in your area, especially if you're going alone and you don't want to rent a room by yourself." Gay ski clubs can also help arrange transportation and perhaps even get better rates.

Resources

Alternative Holidays, (44)(0)20-7701-7040, www.alternative-holidays.com

Aspen Gay Ski Week, 800-367-8290, www.gayskiweek.com

Aspen Ski Tours, 800-367-8290

Gay & Lesbian Ski Week at Whistler Resort, Out on the Slopes Productions, 888-ALTITUDE or 604-688-5079, www.out ontheslopes.com

Lake Tahoe Winterfest, 877-777-4950, www.laketahoewinter
fest.com
Men on Vacation, 888-333-4668
OutWest Global Adventures, 800-743-0458 or 406-446-1533,
www.outwestadventures.com

Riding the Rapids

Whitewater rafting isn't as difficult as it may look.
That's what Leslie says after his two hundred-mile, six-day
group whitewater rafting trip through the Grand Canyon with
Toto Tours.
The trip was so civilized that vacationers didn't even have to
paddle unless they wanted to. "The rafts are pretty large," he
says. "If you want to ride the rapids, you can. It's like sitting on
a wet roller coaster, I guess. But on the back of the raft, it's
quite civilized."
"The raft was a big, motorized kind of thing where we didn't
have to do the paddling," adds Joe, another rafter, from the
same trip. "When there's whitewater, there's a bit of a ride. It's
really quite thrilling. It felt like an adventure, although it was a
safe adventure. The tour company that ran the boat made it
very safe and just the right mix of activity and leisure."
The journey began in Las Vegas, where guests boarded a
small plane for a flight to Lee's Ferry in Marble Canyon, Arizona. After an orientation and overnight stay at the Cliff
Dwellers Lodge, travelers climbed onto one of two fifteen-
passenger rafts for their journey.
"Even the way they got you out there, in a small Cessna
plane, and then being lifted out of the canyon in a helicopter,
was a thrill," Joe says. "In a week's time, you felt like you'd
done more than just go somewhere and be lazy."
Toto Tours actually contracted out to **Hatch River Tours,** a
mainstream rafting company, for the adventure. "The guides
told us that Toto Tours is the most fun group that they do,"
notes Joe.

The days begin with the rising sun and a morning of rafting through gradually changing scenery. "The first two days, you think it all looks the same," recalls Leslie. "But after that, you start to appreciate the differences. The guides tell you about geology and the wildlife, too." As the trip progresses, the walls surrounding the canyon rise to over one mile in height.

Meals were prepared over a propane gas fire, and everyone was responsible for washing his or her own utensils at the end of the meal. "The food that they made was very good, and they were very creative," says Leslie. "They even have ice for your happy hour drinks."

During breaks from the rafting, hiking trips introduce the rafters to the varied landscape of the canyon, which includes lagoons, waterfalls, and even Indian ruins. "You also get to swim a bit and use your muscles," Joe adds.

Although tents were brought along, the weather was agreeable enough for sleeping in the open air. For a fee, the tour operator will provide you with a tarp and air mattress, a sleeping bag, and a pillow, "so you're reasonably comfortable," says Leslie.

Any minor discomfort is worth it, according to Joe, who says that "sleeping under the stars was a wonderful experience."

"It's very different from getting on a plane and going to Hong Kong and doing sight-seeing for a week," says Leslie. "You're in the middle of nowhere, and you don't have all the creature comforts."

"There's definitely some adjustments that take some getting used to," agrees Joe. "Bathing was done in the river, shaving was done in the river. But if you're willing to push the envelope a little bit, it's worth it."

Because of the minimal luxuries included on the trip, Joe says that "the people who do this are more down-to-earth people" than on other trips.

"The tour definitely seems to attract people that are compatible," says Leslie. "What makes this trip special is that you don't realize you're going to be spending so much time with fifteen people, and after a while, you really get to know each other. The group organizer was very good at getting people to interact with each other."

"I had been considering an RSVP-type trip," says Joe, "but I was traveling by myself, and going into a three hundred-person environment can be intimidating. But going into a small group was much easier. This trip was ideal for people who want to travel but don't want to go by themselves or with a huge group of people."

Other rafting trips are available from **OutWest Global Adventures,** which offers a trip to Machu Picchu, Peru, that includes rafting on the Urubamba River. San Francisco-based **Venture Out** offers a "Costa Rican Adventure" itinerary that includes river rafting plus easy hiking explorations in the cloud forest.

If you've mastered river rafting, kayaking will be child's play. Many tour operators offer kayaking.

There are several options for women interested in rafting and other similar activities. **Mariah Wilderness Expeditions** offers women-only trips with whitewater rafting on several California rivers, including the South Fork, Middle Fork, and North Fork of the American River, as well as the Merced, Kings, Kaweah, and Tuolumne River. Mariah also offers soft adventure itineraries to Costa Rica, which include whitewater rafting and sea kayaking; Canada and Baja California are additional destinations that the company features for sea kayaking. Both **Hawk, I'm Your Sister** and **Her Wild Song** offer canoe and kayaking trips in various regions of the U.S., with an emphasis on spirituality and creating a supportive environment (there's more information on these tour operators in the "Special Interest" section).

Resources

Hawk, I'm Your Sister, 505-984-2268, www.womansplace.com
Her Wild Song, 207-721-9005, www.herwildsong.org
Mariah Wilderness Expeditions, 800-462-7424, www.mariah we.com

OutWest Global Adventures, 800-743-0458 or 406-446-1533, www.outwestadventures.com

Toto Tours, 312-274-8686

Hiking the Trails

"All you really need is a comfortable pair of shoes, and you're good to go," says Alexandra, an avid hiking enthusiast.

Well, you probably could do with some clothes, too, plus an itinerary and a place to sleep.

Hiking is one of the most popular outdoor activities and is ideal for many travelers because it doesn't necessarily require the skill, stamina, or experience needed for other types of active vacations such as mountain climbing or bicycling. Many hiking excursions are slow, easy walks through some of the most striking scenery in the world.

It is an activity that is usually incorporated into tours that focus on other activities, as you may have noticed while reading other entries in this chapter.

The western United States is a popular region for hiking.

Earth Walks, based in Santa Fe, New Mexico, offers hiking trips in the the southwestern U.S. and Mexico, providing opportunities to meet with and learn from Native American artists and healers. Activities are for those interested in learning more about the cultural, artistic, and healing traditions of these regions and can be custom-designed for your group. Time is spent in inspirational land settings, and accommodations are camping areas and/or indoor lodging.

Backcountry Tracks is a one-woman, gay- and lesbian-friendly guide service that offers small group excursions in northern California. From December through April, the excursions take the form of snowshoe hiking. Catherine Stifter, the owner, offers some exclusively gay and lesbian trips every year, and can also arrange customized excursions for groups of four or more.

Escalante, Utah-based **Rainbow Country Tours** leads guided trips on foot and by Jeep, exploring canyons, rock formations, and Native American ruins. The company also operates a small bed and breakfast, allowing visitors to tailor the length of their stay and the duration of the hiking and Jeep expeditions.

OutWest Global Adventures offers hiking options in a variety of destinations, from the U.S. Virgin Islands to the Swiss Alps and the ruins of Machu Picchu, Peru.

Alyson Adventures offers trips for hikers of all abilities, including a seven-night excursion to Switzerland that begins in Zermatt, a hub for skiing near the Matterhorn. Heading out from this base, hikers can explore seemingly endless trails through the mountains. The company's "Grindelwald" itinerary, meanwhile, is based in what the tour operator calls "the Switzerland of Heidi," set in a valley marked by meadows of wildflowers, forests and mountain lakes. Alyson's "Tuscan Trails" package features a week of hiking in this fabled region of Italy, visiting ancient towns, vineyards, churches and farms, as well as Etruscan burial mounds dating to 700 B.C.

Adventure Bound Expeditions, based in Boulder, Colorado, has offered a variety of men-only trips that feature hiking, including a recent 16-day trip to the Spanish and French Pyrenees, with ten days of hiking in two national parks, including visits to the walled medieval city of Cascassone in France and Barcelona, Spain.

For women only, **Her Wild Song** offers summer and fall trips in Maine that include hiking and canoeing, as well as a springtime hiking-and-backpacking visit to Escalante National Monument in Utah.

Of course, there are some pretty strenuous hiking trips, in some exotic locations. Mainstream tour operator **Himalayan High Treks** specializes in escorted tours to Nepal, India, Bhutan, and Tibet. Effie Fletcher, the company's owner and frequently a group leader, warns that the trips are "not suitable for those afraid of heights or who don't like to exercise." The trips may begin with comfortable hotel accommodations, but during the actual hiking treks, tents (which are pitched by staff members) are the norm. After a large breakfast at the campsite, the trekking begins, lasting anywhere from two to four hours and resuming again after a long, leisurely lunch. According to Effie, springtime hikes are marked by vibrant wildflowers, while fall provides clear views of the spectacular scenery.

Among the packages offered by Himalayan High Treks, the "Everest Classic" package to Nepal allows visitors to meet Mount Everest face to face.

If you feel like taking a step beyond hiking, how about mountain climbing? Mainstream operator **Mountain Madness** offers excursions to Africa (where you'll get to know Mount Kilimanjaro), Nepal, and the Pacific Northwest.

Regardless of your destination, there are a few essentials you shouldn't forget, regardless of where you're going. Alexandra adds that in addition to a good pair of hiking shoes, "you have to know your limits when setting out. Don't exhaust yourself. Bring lots of water, plus sunblock, comfortable clothes, and bug repellent. And if you're going on a group trip, be sure you know ahead of time what equipment they'll supply."

"When you've got all the right equipment, then just get out there," says Alexandra. "You're going to have the greatest time, especially if you're in a gay group. Experiencing the great outdoors—the fresh air, the scenery, and the exercise, is a wonderful feeling."

Resources

Adventure Bound Expeditions, 303-449-0990, www.adventure boundmen.com

Alyson Adventures, 800-825-9766 or 617-542-1177

Backcountry Tracks, 888-6TRACKS, www.backcountrytracks. com

Earth Walks, 505-988-4157

Himalayan High Treks, 800-455-8735, www.himalayanhigh treks.com

Mountain Madness, 206-937-8389, www.mountainmadness.com

OutWest Global Adventures, 800-743-0458 or 406-543-0262

Rainbow Country Tours, 800-826-4567

TRAVEL TIP

Keeping Up to Date

In addition to the ever-increasing number of Web sites listed elsewhere in this book, several hard-copy periodicals can provide you with regular updates about travel offerings and the gay travel industry in general. Here are some of the best:

Our World   1104 North Nova Rd., Suite 251, Daytona Beach, FL 32117; 904-441-5367. Fax 904-441-5604. $35/10 issues. A glossy publication covering gay and lesbian travel and tours around the world, with lots of photos.

Out & About   995 Market St., San Francisco, CA 94103; 415-644-8044. Website: www.outandabout.com. $49/10 issues. Essential reading for any gay person serious about travel. A well-written, well-researched publication with critical reviews of gay travel experiences.

Passport Magazine   584 Castro St., Suite 521, San Francisco, CA 94114; 800-999-9718. Website: www.passportmagazine.net. $14.95/six issues. The newest entry in the field, Passport is a glossy, full-color magazine that covers a wide variety of topics, including tour packages, business destinations, and independent travel. An entertaining and informative read, and the striking photos make this magazine the most eye-catching.

The Specialist   Community Marketing, Inc., 584 Castro St. #834, San Francisco, CA 94114; 415-437-3800. Fax 415-552-5104. Website: www.mark8ing.com. $29/yr. Basically a trade newsletter for travel professionals, it is nonetheless a source of information that gay and lesbian travelers may find useful.

2

ADVENTURES ABROAD

"Switzerland is my favorite place now,
because it's so—nothing. There's absolutely
nothing to do."

—Andy Warhol

Mr. Warhol definitely was not a travel agent.

Nor was he like the average gay or lesbian traveler, since we tend to approach travel abroad with more enthusiasm than that dear denizen of pop culture. The number of excursions available is proof of our enthusiasm.

Have you ever dreamed of exploring the pyramids of ancient Egypt? Do great theatrical works in London leave you in awe? How about architecture, museums, sociopolitical history—even wildlife? You could explore ancient civilizations or have a wild time learning how the locals have fun. The travel packages for gay people are broad in both subject matter and geographic region.

When deciding on a vacation abroad, destinations like Amsterdam, London, and Montreal quickly come to mind, because of their large gay and lesbian populations and the wide variety of accommodations and activities for gay people. In cities like these, we feel welcome and don't experience too much culture shock trying to adjust to our surroundings.

But every continent on this planet has something to offer the gay or lesbian traveler, whether you're in an escorted tour or making your own arrangements. What you'll read in this chapter is but a sample of some of the escorted and independent tours offered.

THINGS TO THINK ABOUT FIRST   What part of travel interests you most—going out, being with friends, meeting people, architecture, politics, people, the fine arts? What regions in the world interest you? Which tours would devote attention to your favorite destinations and subject areas? Make sure that there will be enough time for you to see what's important to you.

QUESTIONS TO ASK THE TRAVEL PROVIDER   What is the focus of the trips offered, and what is the range of destinations? What activities are planned? What is the tour guide's background and how knowledgeable is he/she about the destination(s) as well as gay and lesbian culture? Are the destinations homophobic or dangerous at all, and how does the tour handle this? What climate(s) will be visited and what are the appropriate clothing and supplies to bring? What is included in the cost—meals, airfare, ground transportation to and from the airport, activities and admission to various events and facilities? What are the accommodations like and where are they located in relation to attractions/activities/nightlife? Are refunds guaranteed in case of cancellation? How much time will we have to explore each location we visit? How much time will we have on our own? Is nightlife included in the tour?

Some Countries Are Friendlier Than Others

In the early 1990s, the Netherlands launched an historic advertising campaign that included magazine ads targeted at lesbian and gay travelers. It was the first time the government of any nation had actively courted the gay market.

The Netherlands continues to welcome us in a big way—they even hosted the Gay Games in 1998. But the variety of countries interested in attracting gay and lesbian visitors has increased in a major way. Today, there are gay promotional efforts officially sanctioned by local and national governments in places like Great Britain, Canada, Australia, France, and the Scandinavian countries (this increase has been matched by a greater number of U.S. tourism organizations courting the gay market—places as varied as Providence, Rhode Island and Rochester, N.Y.). A visit to any **Gay and Lesbian World Travel Expo** (organized by San Francisco-based Community Marketing) or a convention of the **International Gay and Lesbian Travel Association** provides a glimpse of even more destinations that are looking into the benefits of courting the gay market. The tourism organizations of Puerto Rico and Hong Kong, for example, have increased their presence in the gay travel market and are organizing their efforts. Many destinations, where the government might not officially encourage gay tourism, are nevertheless well covered in terms of privately owned infrastructure (gay and lesbian bars, hotels and other businesses) and tour operators.

Mexico, for example, is one of the most popular international destinations for straight people from the United States. It is also a favorite for gay tour operators, and independent gay and lesbian travelers have found an amazing variety of affordable vacation options with our neighbor to the south: from the museums and urban nightlife of Mexico City, to the Mayan and Aztec ruins scattered throughout the country, to the sun-drenched beaches of cities like Cancun and Acapulco.

Puerto Vallarta, on the Pacific coast, is being promoted by **Doin' It Right Travel** as the most gay-friendly destination in Mexico, with a selection of accommodations and a respectable number of gay nightspots. **Olivia Cruises and Resorts** offers a women-only week at the Club Med Sonora Bay, **Atlantis** has an all-gay week at a resort in Puerto Vallarta, and **RSVP Vacations** has offered an all-gay all-inclusive week at the Club Med in Cancun, as well as cruises to Mexico's Pacific Coast from Los Angeles.

Arco Iris offers a variety of tours to Mexico, including Puerto Vallarta, Guadalajara, Mardi Gras in Veracruz, Mexico City during gay pride week, the Cancun International Gay Festival, and an "X-rated," men-only party in Cozumel.

We gay people patronize nations across the globe. Why haven't more of them spent money trying to attract us? The probable reasons are ignorance, a small advertising budget, and perhaps prejudice.

This doesn't mean, of course, that you can't have a gay old time in just about any nation in the world (or at least a good number of them). Individual businesses thrive globally by serving gay and lesbian tourists. It's just that most government tourism offices don't have a clue about the importance and needs of lesbian and gay travelers.

By the time you read this, more governments may be courting our tourist dollars. Look for their ads in gay publications, and remember that the ones who woo us will probably treat us better as visitors—or at least listen to us more attentively.

In the meantime, let's take a look at some of the countries that appreciate us the most.

The Netherlands

Amsterdam's liberalism goes all the way back to the city's prosperity during the Golden Age of 1580 to 1720, when immigrants of many backgrounds began arriving in this beautiful city. Today, you can enjoy the artwork of Dutch Old Masters, visit the homes of Rembrandt and Anne Frank, stroll down the banks of the city's many canals, and admire historic architecture. A sobering visit to the Homo-monument, a tribute to gay people everywhere, is sure to make you pause and recognize the depth of our struggle, as well as how much the Netherlands respects that struggle.

Of course, Amsterdam's reputation for wild nightlife is another big draw for gays and lesbians. The seemingly endless number of bars and discos caters to a diverse clientele from around the world. It's easy to get the impression that Amsterdam is where Europeans come to party.

Of the many special events that take place throughout the year, the birthday of Queen Juliana, and the gigantic Queen's Day celebration on April 30, is one of the most gay-popular holidays in Europe. The streets of Amsterdam fill with revelers for more than twenty-four hours of street fairs, markets, music, and food. Of course, the gay bars are packed.

Considering how much the Netherlands has done to make us feel welcome, it's no surprise that several tour operators offer gay package deals.

Above and Beyond offers a Thanksgiving trip to Amsterdam (where, by the way, there is no Thanksgiving holiday). Included in the Thanksgiving trip are an escorted evening club tour, a gay welcome packet, a city orientation tour, and accommodations at a hotel centrally located for exploring the vibrant gay nightlife. Above and Beyond also offers a "Queens Day Amsterdam" package that features the parades, live music, and parties of this national holiday. Also included are a gay welcome packet, a guided bar tour with welcome cocktails, a tour of Keukenhof Tulip Gardens with lunch, and the services of local, English-speaking gay guides. Above and Beyond also offers Business Class packages, in conjunction with United Airlines, to Amsterdam (as well as other European destinations). The three-night Amsterdam package includes roundtrip business class transportation on United, three nights at the Barbizon Palace hotel, daily breakfast, a gay welcome packet, a half-day city tour, entrance to Rijksmuseum (a well-known museum in the city), and the services of a local gay tour operator.

Amsterdam is designated one of the "Gay & Lesbian Capitals of Europe" according to German mega-airline **Lufthansa**, which publishes a guide to some of the continent's most gay-friendly destinations.

Australia

While the lesbian and gay community is well established in many parts of the nation down under, the gay hub of the country is generally considered to be Sydney, where the ever-popular Oxford Street is lined with gay-owned businesses. It is here that Australia's best-known gay and lesbian event, the Mardi Gras, is held every year, drawing thousand of participants from across the country and abroad. The celebration lasts an entire month and includes theater, music, sports, and many, many social events. The climax of the celebration is the massive parade, which boasts well over ten thousand participants every year.

That's far from the only event in Australia—the Sleaze Ball, held in September or October, is another popular annual party that raises funds for various organizations. In the fall of 2002, Sydney joined the list of gay-friendly destinations that have hosted Gay Games.

There is an abundance of tour operators anxious to offer up packages in conjunction with Sydney's gay and lesbian celebrations. But don't forget that there's plenty to see outside of Sydney—and there are several packages that can help you see it.

Above and Beyond Tours offers an extensive program of tours to Australia. The company offers four different packages for Mardi Gras. The "Tale of Three Cities" package is an escorted tour that includes three nights in Auckland, New Zealand, with attendance at the HERO fair, part of a three-week celebration of sporting events, film festivals, theater, and arts. From there, group members fly to Melbourne, Australia for a two-night visit and finally a five-night visit to Sydney for the big Mardi Gras celebration, including wine tasting, a gay harbor cruise, a "gay swim carnival" and plenty of opportunities to party.

Above and Beyond's "V.I.P." and "Budget Buster" packages are, respectively, upscale and discounted packages—both of which are escorted—to Sydney's Mardi Gras. And the company's sweeping "Best of the South Pacific" package is a four-week blockbuster that takes in 23 hotel nights, eight destinations, and 30 meals. It incorporates other existing itineraries including the "Tale of Three Cities," mentioned earlier, a more extensive tour of New Zealand, and a visit to the Australian city of Cairns and the Outback for Alice Springs' own gay pride party.

Canada

For decades, our neighbor to the north has been the setting for many a successful gay vacation. Canada's proximity and similarity to the United States make it one of the most convenient foreign countries to visit, and the array of activities and attractions is impressive.

Without a doubt, the most popular gay destination for men is Montreal, where the city's Village district pumps with dance music every night of the week and a permissive atmosphere allows for wild times. Shopping, museums, and festivals fill the daylight hours (when the cold winter sets in, underground malls and passageways allow for warmth and mobility).

Because Canada is our next-door neighbor, most people make their own plans to visit independently. But air and land packages may help make vacations more affordable. **Divers/ Cité**, Montreal's lesbian, gay, bisexual, and transgendered pride organization, features ten days of indoor and outdoor activities, including concerts, cultural activities, a community day, and a pride parade.

Outside of the largest urban areas like Montreal, Toronto, and Vancouver, Canada is known for its natural resources, which make for rewarding outdoor-style vacations. If you've ever dreamed of getting to know the great outdoors, Canada is a great place to do it.

Resources

Above and Beyond Tours, 800-397-2681, www.abovebeyond tours.com

Alyson Adventures, 800-825-9766 or 617-247-8170, www. alysonadventures.com

Arco Iris, 800-765-4370, www.arcoiristours.com

Atlantis Events, 800-628-5268, www.atlantisevents.com

Divers/Cité, www.diverscite.org

Doin' It Right Travel, 800-936-DOIN or 619-297-3642, www. doinitright.com

International Gay and Lesbian Travel Association, 800-448-8550 or 954-776-2626, www.iglta.org
  Men on Vacation, 800-959-4636 or 619-298-2285
  Olivia Cruises and Resorts, 800-631-6277 or 510-655-0364
  RSVP Travel Productions, 800-328-RSVP, www.rsvp.net
  Toto Tours, 312-274-TOTO

Exploring Central America

The strangest thing about Costa Rica was that I'd never heard anything bad about it. Every single person I'd spoken with who has visited this little Central American nation has simply *loved* it. *Come on,* I started thinking, *there's gotta be something bad about this place!*

I found out that it isn't easy to speak in negatives about Costa Rica, whether you're straight or gay. Even though Costa Rica may not be as advanced as the Netherlands when it comes to officially welcoming gay and lesbian travelers, it has nevertheless become a favorite destination for thousands of us every year.

"The reason why I think people love it is there's a lot to do, and it's all close by," reasons J. J., who's visited twice from his home in San Francisco. "You can go to two coasts— the Caribbean and the Pacific—in a matter of hours, and the beaches are spectacular. Plus, you can be on the beach on the coast and then go river rafting. There are things like volcanoes and a rain forest. And they have great national parks."

Nearly 30 percent of the country is under protected status. The Monteverde Cloud Forest Reserve is a 2,800-acre private reserve in the highlands of the Tilaran mountains, with unique flora and fauna. The mile-long Rain Forest Aerial Tram allows visitors to see the rain forest from ground level to the top. "It's really cool. It's very colorful. You can see lots of monkeys and animals."

Another selling point is the people. "It hasn't been overgrown with tourists," notes J. J., "and the people are really nice." Costa Rica also benefits from its reputation as the most politically stable nation in Central America—unlike its neighbors, Costa Rica doesn't even have an army, leading some people to call it "the Switzerland of the Americas."

The destination also has a fair selection of gay-friendly hotels and some nightlife, although most visitors come to enjoy its nature more than its nightlife. "I wasn't looking to go out," notes J. J. "I wanted to see the wildlife and enjoy the water. We stayed one time in a big hotel and then another time we stayed in the city of San Jose at a bed and breakfast with parakeets, and it was really cool."

But *come on.* There's got to be something bad you can say about Costa Rica! "Well," J. J. thinks for a minute. "The roads are pretty bad. And my Uncle Bill fell into a crater when he was there, and broke his rib."

J. J. traveled there on his own, but there are gay and lesbian escorted tours available from several companies. For women only, **Mariah Wilderness Expeditions** offers active vacations in Costa Rica that incudes rafting, sea kayaking, and hiking.

Toto Tours' "Rich Coast" escorted tour features visits to Manuel Antonio National Park, where monkeys, sloths, opossums and agouti, as well as hundreds of species of birds, make their home.

Vacationers on the Toto tour can also canoe in the crater of an extinct volcano, witness the eruptions of an active one, and have the option of rafting the whitewater of the Rio Sarapiqui. They can see the annual pilgrimage of giant leatherback turtles, who lay their eggs on Tamarindo Beach. The tour intentionally avoids the popular Monteverde Cloud Forest Reserve, opting for the lesser-known Santa Elena Reserve, where, Toto reasons, fewer tourists means a greater chance of seeing some exciting wildlife, such as the stunning quetzal bird.

Toto also leaves time to explore the city of San Jose, where theater, art, and gay nightlife come together.

Above and Beyond Tours offers a nine-day "Costa Rica Explorer" package several times a year that includes a visit to the capital city, San José; the canals of Tortuguero; the Arenal

Volcano; and Quepos, a popular gay beach area that is also home to Manuel Antonio National Park.

Toronto-based **Footprints** offers a 10-day Costa Rica itinerary, as well as an optional four-day beach extension. **Mariah Wilderness Expeditions** offers customized vacation travel planning for people interested in Costa Rica, with a variety of soft adventure activities, including rainforest hiking, mountain biking, sea kayaking, scuba diving, snorkeling, surfing, and whitewater rafting. They also offer women-only, fully escorted tours to Costa Rica; one of the offerings focuses on exploring volcanoes, cloudforests and beaches, while the other is a multi-sport adventure involving many of the activities mentioned earlier.

Way to Go Costa Rica, a North Carolina-based tour operator specializing in mainstream tours to Costa Rica, has also offered gay and lesbian escorted tours. Accommodations are generally in small, well-appointed hotels with full amenities and, in the case of some properties, a swimming pool and/or Jacuzzi. Among the offerings is a "Tropical Adventure Tour" that includes snorkeling, canoeing, river floating down the Corobici River, horseback riding, and hiking at the Valle Escondido Private Reserve, plus visits to the active Arenal Volcano.

The "Caribbean Escorted Tour" explores the Tortuguero area, along the northeastern Caribbean coastline, with cruises through canals, visits to the beaches of Punta Uvas and, of course, a visit to the Arenal Volcano.

While Costa Rica is unmistakably Central America's leading gay destination, other nations are growing in popularity for many of the same reasons that made Costa Rica popular.

Belize, which shares borders with Mexico and Guatemala, is positioning itself as the "ecocultural destination of the twenty-first century," and with good reason. This nation, formerly known as British Honduras, boasts the largest barrier reef in this hemisphere, in addition to tempting Caribbean beaches. Reasonably priced, small lodging is available on the atolls offshore, where you can easily set off for some spectacular diving and snorkeling. Make friends with the sharks, explore the reef, and enjoy yourself.

The TV program "Temptation Island" has perhaps done more than anything else to publicize the natural wonders of Belize. San Pedro, a formerly quiet fishing village, is a good base for exploring some of the underwater wonders of Ambergris Cay.

Inland, massive ruins from centuries-old Mayan cities dot the lush green forests. Xunantunich, a major ceremonial center, boasts what is still one of the nation's highest structures.

The animals are also an attraction. A visit to the small but fascinating Belize Zoo will give you a quick introduction to the varied species native to the land, including the tapir, which is the national animal. Other spots of interest to nature fans are the Community Baboon Sanctuary, the Crooked Tree Wildlife Sanctuary, and the Cockscomb Basin Wildlife Sanctuary.

Granted, Belize has nothing to offer in terms of gay-specific accommodations, but the relaxed, friendly attitude of the people, coupled with the activities and attractions along the shore and inland, have drawn the attention of a growing number of gay and lesbian travelers.

Of course, you can make your visit to Belize gayer by joining a gay tour. **Undersea Expeditions** also offers scuba-diving trips to Belize, with comfortable, live-aboard boats that serve as a base for exploring the colorful reef. Undersea's annual Thanksgiving trip to Belize includes seven nights aboard the Wave Dancer, in cabins with private baths, up to five dives daily, including a night dive every night; all meals, snacks and beverages, and even turkey on the reef on Thanksgiving day.

Footprints offers a 13-day excursion to Belize including a three-day excursion across the Guatemalan border to Tikal, where visitors explore one of the best-known Mayan ruins. **Adventures in Good Company** offers a "Best of Belize" program, for women only, that includes snorkeling, scuba diving, and exploring Mayan ruins.

Another Central American option is Honduras. **Undersea Expeditions** offers a seven-night, men-only package to the Inn of Last Resort, a gay-friendly property on the northwest coast of Roatan, Honduras. Here, guest can take easy dives and see sponges and coral. Included are five days of boat dives, including one night dive, as well as breakfast, lunch and dinner daily, unlimited daytime shore diving, a "get-acquainted" cocktail party, use of mask, fins and snorkel, and other amenities.

Another great option is Guatemala, which has a countryside dotted with Mayan ruins, picturesque towns, mountains and volcanoes, as well as a capital city with a lively gay nightlife. **Coda International Tours** offers a 10-day "Guatemala at Christmas" tour that includes three nights in the beautiful colonial town of Antigua, visit to the famous arts-and-crafts market at Chichicastenango, a cruise on Lake Atitlán, and a visit to the Mayan ruins at Tikal. The final night is spent in gay hub Guatemala City.

There are plenty of other places to discover in Central America. Panama City boasts an active gay nightlife as well as modern amenities and easy access to the Panama Canal and beautiful ecotourism spots elsewhere in the country. **Cruising With Pride** has offered a gay group cruise of the Panama Canal.

And, of course, your own traveling can take you wherever you want to go in the region. There is plenty of nonstop airline service from U.S. gateways to the largest cities in Central America, and airlines including American, Continental, COPA (of Panama) and Grupo TACA (which is a collection of four Central American airlines) offer independent vacation packages to the most popular destinations. TACA also offers a "Latin AirFlex" program that provides discounted airfare for personalized itineraries within Central America.

Resources

Adventures in Good Company, 651-998-0120 or 877-439-4042, www.good adventure.com

Coda International Tours, 888-677-2632, www.coda-tours.com

Cruising With Pride, 866-200-2086, www.cruisingwithpride.com

Footprints, 888-962-6211 or 416-962-8111, www.footprints travel.com

Mariah Wilderness Expeditions, 800-4-MARIAH, www.mariah we.com

Toto Tours, 312-274-TOTO, www.tototours.com

Undersea Expeditions, 800-669-0310, www.underseax.com

Way to Go Costa Rica, 800-835-1223, www.waytogocosta rica.com

---

TRAVEL TIP

Finding a Good Travel Agent

The truth is, you don't *have* to go through a travel agent in order to get the best deals or to find details about vacation packages. Especially thanks to the Internet, doing research and even booking travel has become as easy as sitting down at your keyboard.

But many people aren't willing to do all the work and research to make informed decisions—so they'd rather use the services of a travel professional. In many cases, travel agents can make your trip go smoother and save you time and money. They've got more experience than most of us in weaving through complex airfares, sorting out package deals, and matching travelers with hotel rooms.

A travel agent who's knowledgeable about gay and lesbian travel can be even more helpful. Not only do savvy agents save you money on airfare and package deals, they can help you find gay-friendly accommodations and will be up to date on the latest tours and cruises. They'll know when and where the best parties are in South Beach, as well as which frequent flyer program lets you share mileage with your significant other.

Travel agents have far outpaced other travel businesses in responding to the needs of gay and lesbian travelers. This may be because a larger number of agents and agency owners are openly gay than other industry professionals. Not that an agent *has* to be gay to serve your travel needs. But it helps to have a familiarity with the market and gay travel options.

The key is to find a good travel agent, because as in any industry, there are plenty of bad eggs who would rather throw a brochure at you and book you on the first flight that comes

up on their computer. The best way to find an effective agent
is by word of mouth—ask your friends who travel a lot if
they're pleased with their travel agent. In today's world of
toll-free phone numbers, you're no longer restricted to agencies in your general vicinity. Large and small agencies across
the country are waiting to serve your needs.

Another way is by looking in any gay publication. It's
almost guaranteed you'll see some ads for travel agencies.
Some are small, storefront operations, while others are massive franchises.

How can you tell who really knows their stuff? Telltale
signs include membership in the International Gay and Lesbian Travel Association or the Travel Alternatives Group, or
advertisements in the gay press.

But don't stop there. Call up the agency yourself and ask
them a few questions. How much experience do they have
with the gay market? What kind of travel do they specialize in
and what services do they offer? Is there a fee for any of the
services?

You should also be clear about your own personal travel
preferences, especially once it comes time to plan your trip.
The more your agent knows about you, the better he or she
can hook you up with your dream vacation. Even if you're not
sure where you want to go or what you want to do, you
should be able to help your agent come up with some appropriate ideas. What kind of weather and destinations do you
prefer? What activities interest you? What is your budget for
the trip and how much time do you have to take it? What frequent flyer programs do you belong to? A good agent will pay
close attention to your preferences and should know what
types of vacations are most likely to please you.

For referrals to gay and gay-friendly travel agencies in your
area, call the International Gay and Lesbian Travel Association at 800-448-8550 or visit www.iglta.org.

Around the World With Hanns

Hanns Ebensten, who pioneered the gay tour market with a
trip to Colorado Springs in the 1970s, has been leading gay
tours longer than just about anyone. Dr. Sam J. Little and his

partner, David Martin, took their first trip with Hanns Ebensten, to Carnival in Rio de Janeiro, in the mid-eighties. "We enjoyed that so much, we've done a trip almost once a year," says Sam, who lives in Oklahoma City. "We've been to Greece, Russia, Thailand. We did his twentieth anniversary around the world. We did the Orient Express."

In 2001, Hanns Ebensten sold his company, Hanns Ebensten Travel. But he still leads some tours himself, and the company still focuses on the same type of travel.

Sam and David have come to prefer these cultural tours. Sam says he appreciates the fact that Ebensten's groups are relatively small. "They're small groups—sometimes as few as half a dozen," he reports. "For us, that's a very congenial and cozy group to travel with. We just returned from Australia, from a Men on Vacation tour, which is a different kind of tour. They had three hundred men coming in."

Indeed, cultural tours usually attract a different type of traveler than party-oriented trips. "Hanns's groups tend to be more mature people," Sam continues. "I'm in my sixties and my partner is in his fifties. We enjoy Hanns more because of the suitability of the age group and the nature of the trips. It's more geared toward culture."

Sam and David also like the variety built into each trip. Meals, for example, are served in some of the finest establishments, as well as in more ordinary settings where locals congregate. "It's fascinating. You get to see a little bit of everything."

Knowledgeable guides are on hand to make sure you get the most out of your experience. "When Hanns is on a trip, he has experts in whatever historical or archaeological area you're visiting, so when we were in Egypt with him, we had Egyptian experts at the pyramids."

According to Sam, Ebensten's groups are made up primarily of single gay men. Some trips are offered every year, others only occasionally. "I don't think we've ever been anywhere with Hanns that he hadn't been before," says Sam. "He does an extremely good job at what he's offering."

Hanns offers trips to a wide variety of destinations, including mysterious Easter Island, a small island in the middle of the South Pacific that is home to hundreds of ancient stone statues, the exact history of which may never be known. Travelers venture up the Rano Kau Volcano, for a look down into its crater lake, and inspect other regions of cultural interest, such as the old ceremonial village of Orongo, which still boasts large basalt rocks decorated with markings of birdmen and of the god *Make-Make*.

The Nile cruises, which vary in terms of itinerary and accommodations, offer visitors the chance to explore the Egyptian cities of Cairo, Aswan, and Luxor, while taking in the monuments representing the majesty of Pharaonic, classic and early Christian, medieval, and Muslim cultures. The cruising has been offered in both felucca sailboats and in paddle steamers—both of which are designed to escape the massive crush of tourists that sometimes invade these popular destinations.

Hanns's cruise up the Amazon River features daily and nocturnal explorations in small boats and on foot into the lush jungles of the region. Other selections include cultural tours of Thailand, a Christmas visit to Marrakech, and cruises to the Galápagos Islands, home of an array of wildlife that greatly influenced Charles Darwin's theories.

Resources

Hanns Ebensten Travel, 305-294-8174 or 866-294-8174, www. hetravel.com

African Safaris

"Camping in Africa was an experience," Daniel recalls after a recent safari expedition. "The campfires were fun, but the lions roaring and the elephants trumpeting at night made it hard to sleep." At least that's insomnia he'll not soon forget.

It's also the kind of vacation that can only be had in Africa, a continent that still remains mysterious to most Eurocentric travelers.

Daniel, who hails from Milwaukee, visited Tanzania with **Toto Tours,** taking in the snow-capped peak of Kilimanjaro and the wildlife of the Serengeti.

In addition to spending some nights camping in the great wilderness, the group spent several nights at lodges with full amenities, so not every night was interrupted by animal concerts.

"It was an interesting land, and the animals were fascinating," Daniel says. "There were parts that were absolutely breathtaking, some of the best scenery and geography in the world. And the rest of the tour members—there was a total of seven—were great people."

That's a significant endorsement from someone like Daniel, who'd traveled a lot independently, but never on a tour.

"My reservation about traveling in a group is that I like to do my own thing, and I wasn't sure I wanted to be confined to a group. But doing the plains on an African safari, you just can't do it outside of a group. There was airfare and safari and lodging and food. It was complete."

Daniel says going with a gay group was important to him because he wanted to have something in common with his fellow travelers. "That's why I chose it. I didn't want to be three weeks in Africa with the blue-haired people."

The daily schedule focuses on seeing as much of the countryside as possible. "You basically got up at six-thirty, and were in the safari vehicles by eight, chasing animals."

The chase, of course, didn't result in any harm being done to the animals. The closest thing to trophies that the travelers brought home were some excellent wildlife photographs.

"There were numerous animals, such as giraffes and zebras and wildebeests that you see stampede. The vehicle would quietly go into different areas looking for rarer animals like cheetahs, lions. Some animals got very jittery and bolted, some ignored you; they were so big and powerful they didn't mind you approaching."

Daniel says some of the best times were had "getting to know the rest of the tour members during the early evening social hours and the morning safari ventures." Some of the people on the tour have even discussed going to India together.

While there is usually no strenuous activity involved in this kind of tour, Daniel notes that in order to enjoy an African safari, "you have to be fairly adventuresome, flexible, probably have to have traveled a bit. It's not a party atmosphere." Someone who enjoys animals, nature, and photography would also find lots to write home about.

"Roughing it" on the African plain made Daniel appreciate the creature comforts of big-city living, which he was reintroduced to during a two-day stopover at Amsterdam. "It was a relief," he says.

Other tours of the African continent are available from a variety of suppliers. **Coda International Tours** offers a trip to Tanzania and Zanzibar, as well as a 13-day "Treasures of Egypt and the Red Sea" itinerary, which includes five nights aboard a 34-passenger cruise ship on the Red Sea, and visits to several ancient sites, such as Petra, the pyramids, Luxor, and Thebes. Off the coast of Africa, Coda offers a seven-night cruise among the Seychelles, with visits to many of the islands.

David Tours offers a 16-day trip to South Africa, Victoria Falls (in Zambia), and Botswana, an itinerary that includes visits to the wine country around Cape Town, a private game reserve, and optional activities like waterskiing and hang gliding. The company also offers a 16-day Tanzania trip that takes in the Serengeti National Park, staying at game lodges, and a four-night stay on the island of Zanzibar. There is also time to explore Nairobi, Kenya. David Tours explores Kenya even further in a separate, 16-day itinerary that visits the Masai Mara Game Reserve and Amboseli National Park, which has great views of Mount Kilimanjaro. This itinerary also includes a visit to the island of Zanzibar. David Tours clients can explore another part of the continent on the company's eight-day trip to Morocco, which includes one night in Casablanca, three nights in Fez, and three nights in Marrakech.

Resources

Coda International Tours, 888-677-2632, www.coda-tours.com
David Tours, 888-723-0699, www.davidtours.com
Toto Tours, 800-565-1241 or 773-274-8686, www.tototours.com

How Fast Should You Go? Whirlwind vs. Focused Tours of Europe

How best to see the world—in a whirlwind, multicountry tour, or by visiting one country at a time?

It depends on how much you've already traveled, how much time you have, and your own personal preferences.

For Fredda Rubin and her lover, Katia Soares Netto, a multicountry trip was perfect. They traveled with an escorted tour to Portugal, Spain, and Morocco. "We decided to take that tour because neither one of us had been in Europe," says Fredda. "It gave us a wonderful exposure to three countries, plus Gibraltar. Even though our stays were short—eleven hotels in fifteen days, plus seventeen rolls of film—it made us realize where we wanted to go back to."

The trip, which was Fredda's fiftieth birthday present from her lover, included visits to the monasteries of Lisbon, an ancient Roman bridge in Córdoba, and Madrid's Prado museum, home of some of Goya's great masterpieces. In Seville, they visited the cathedral where the tomb of Christopher Columbus lies, and in Tangier, they shopped at the bustling Grand Socco Market and marveled at the Forbes museum; they even stopped for lunch one day in Casablanca.

"At first we were afraid of Morocco," Fredda recalls, "because we know how misogynous they are. But we had a wonderful guide who was there to protect us; they would hire individual guides in each place we were in."

Fredda notes that one advantage of taking a "whirlwind" tour is that you can visit regions that otherwise wouldn't attract a gay and lesbian tour. "I would really love to see more of Portugal," she says, "but unfortunately, there aren't enough people like us to demand that."

One of the countries that *does* generate sufficient gay interest is Greece, which was the focus of a tour that a traveler named Tony took. Tony had taken a multicountry tour before, but didn't like it as much. "It was tiring," he says now. "And it was too busy. They got you up at seven. It was a bus trip from Amsterdam to Venice and back through France. The people on the trip were very nice, but not very sophisticated. It was one day in the Netherlands, one day in Venice, one day in Paris, one day in Germany."

Part of the problem, he says, was that "it was the same people on the bus, day after day. On the Greek trip, we were just one more group in a much larger group, in the context of a much larger ship."

Still, he says, "if you've never been abroad, [a whirlwind tour is] a great introduction. It's a way of discovering where you want to go back to."

Tony's trip to Greece (with a side trip to Turkey) was much slower paced than this earlier tour. They spent a total of seven days on a ship, plus two nights in Athens and an optional three nights on the Greek island of Mykonos.

Given the historical popularity of homosexual activity usually attributed to Greece, it may seem logical that the nation still is a popular gay destination. But Tony warns that the sense of history is fairly limited. "There's obviously that historic tradition, but I don't think it's much of a part of life today," he says. "There is a fair amount of homoerotic pottery—four-inch statues with eight-inch dicks. There's pottery with men performing fellatio and sodomy. Several people bought some as souvenirs."

Clearly, it is more than homoerotic pottery that continues to draw homosexual travelers to Greece. A rich culture and historically significant architecture are part of the attraction; gorgeous beaches, reasonable prices, and an active gay scene are others.

"I thought the Greece tour was wonderful," says Tony. "There were three stages: we were in Athens, then we were on a very nice cruise ship. I love cruising, and I love the idea of being carried from one place to another without packing and unpacking."

The twenty-six-person group began this journey in Athens, Greece, with tours of historic sites like the Parthenon (Tony notes that it cost extra to visit some of the ruins).

Accommodations were extremely pleasant. "In Athens, we had a very nice suite with a balcony and a view of the Parthenon." He especially liked the Mykonos accommodation. "Our room overlooked a very large swimming pool and patio, and just beyond was the Aegean." Still, he says, "I don't know that Mykonos is any more beautiful than any other Greek island. They're all beautiful. What Mykonos has is nightlife and tons of gorgeous boys and girls."

He and his lover didn't necessarily partake in that nightlife, though. "We are not night people. Some people are, and in Athens and Mykonos, they went out to gay bars. I'm a theater person. We didn't even go into town to eat dinner, because there were a string of low-key, moderately priced restaurants near the beaches."

Next, they sailed into the Aegean Sea, stopping at the Greek islands of Santorini, Crete, Rhodes, and Patmos. Then it was time to enter Turkey, through the port of Kusadasi. A day of sight-seeing in Istanbul was included.

The gay group functioned well within the context of larger mainstream groups, according to Tony, although he notes that his group was "much more lively than most Globus tours. The guide we had in Greece was young and hip and enjoyed herself with us."

So what's the difference whether you book with a mainstream or gay group? "It's a world of difference. If my lover and I had booked with [a mainstream group], whether we were made to feel that way or not, we would feel self-conscious about being two men traveling alone. When we travel with [people like us], we're part of a gay group. It's being with your own people. Whenever we wanted to hold hands, we held hands."

There is one problem that could face any traveler, gay or straight. "The drawback is that there's bound to be one or two obnoxious people," Tony recalls. "On this last trip, one guy traveling had diarrhea of the mouth and was not sensitive to other people's reactions."

So it was a saving grace that most of the trip took place on a rather large ship. "We weren't cooped together much," Tony says. The only risky time was at dinner, when people were grouped together at smaller tables. "My lover said, 'If he's sitting at my table, I'm getting up.'" And once, they ended up doing just that. "But that's the only time we had to deal with it."

Even with the risk of obnoxious travelers, Tony says that group tours are the best way to see many destinations. "The reason we were on tours to begin with is I'm a very timid traveler. I don't like to be in countries where English isn't spoken, so I don't know if I'd ever get to Venice on my own."

You can see Greece and Turkey with several gay tour operators. **Above and Beyond Tours** offers a "Tropical Mykonos" packages that includes a half-day Mykonos city tour, a beach barbecue, a day tour to Delos, and five nights of hotel accommodations. The company also offers a "Turkish Delight" itinerary that includes five nights at a four-star hotel, a full-day private tour of Istanbul, with visits to the Roman Hippodrome, the Blue Mosque, the Topkapi Palace, St. Sophia, the Grand Bazaar, and a 300-year-old Turkish bath. Also included is a cruise on the Bosphorus to the Asian side, with a visit to the nineteenth-century Beylerbeyi Palace and Sadberk Hanim museum.

Whether taking a whirlwind tour or focusing on one or two hot spots, the variety of tour operators is impressive.

For the active-minded, **Alyson Adventures, Toto Tours,** and **Progressive Travels** offer the chance to see Europe from the seat of a bicycle. Their cycling tours cover various itineraries in western Europe.

Atlas Global Services has teamed up with gay and lesbian tour operators in Spain and Russia for various tour packages (the company offers independent travel packages for destinations around the world).

An interesting way to get to know a foreign country is by visiting it during special events and celebrations. Gay and lesbian pride celebrations take place in most western European countries (frequently in more than one city), and there are other festivals and events scheduled throughout the year. Tour operators frequently offer package deals to these events, but it may be just as easy to visit independently. What better way to see how people live than to watch them party?

Resources

Above and Beyond Tours, 800-397-2681, www.abovebeyond tours.com

Alyson Adventures, 800-825-9766 or 617-247-8170, www. alysonadventures.com

Progressive Travels, 800-245-2229

Toto Tours, 800-565-1241 or 773-274-8686, www.tototours.com

Caribbean Getaways

For straight people, the Caribbean is a wide-open playground, filled with fun, relaxation, and romance. Gay people may have to be more selective when choosing a Caribbean destination, because several islands have a reputation for being homophobic.

Still, a growing number of hotels and resorts (mostly smaller, privately owned ones) are sprouting up throughout the Caribbean that are eager to serve us. And several destinations offer gay nightlife.

Still, in terms of established, U.S.-style gay and lesbian life, most of the islands don't have much of an infrastructure. Puerto Rico is the only example of an island with a wide array of U.S.-style clubs, bars, hotels, and guest houses for gays and lesbians.

As in the rest of the world, homophobia is a problem in the Caribbean, and acceptance of alternative lifestyles varies widely from island to island. Generally, the nations associated with the former British Empire (i.e., most of the English-speaking islands) have the worst reputation for intolerance. The moral system instilled by our friends in Victorian England still influences modern society, and while an underground gay scene may exist on an island like Jamaica, the gay community is fairly closed and is not easy to track down if you don't have an "inside" contact.

But you can still enjoy the Caribbean sun and surf, romance, and maybe even nightlife, depending on what kind of vacation you're looking for. I've broken this section down into two categories: romance and partying, since most travelers to the Caribbean are looking for one or both of these experiences.

Of course, there are other reasons to visit the Caribbean islands. Many gay and lesbian travelers enjoy the region's outstanding beaches, cultural attractions, and water sports like scuba diving and snorkeling. But look beyond just the underwater activities, because even though places like Jamaica and the Cayman Islands offer outstanding aquatics, they generally don't extend a friendly welcome to gay and lesbian travelers (there are exceptions, as you'll find when you read on). Saba, on the other hand, boasts great diving *and* gay-friendly accommodations.

Various tour operators offer escorted tours to Caribbean islands. New York City-based **Amigos Tours** operates escorted tours to the Dominican Republic, including visits to the capital city of Santo Domingo as well as several of the beautiful beach resorts. The company can also make arrangements for independent travel to the Dominican Republic, offering suggestions for gay-friendly accommodations and activities.

Alyson Adventures has offered a package called "An Octopus's Garden," a diving-oriented trip to Saba that includes 12 dives over the course of five days for certified divers, or lessons for beginners, followed by actual diving. **Atlantis Events** and **Olivia Cruises and Resorts** both offer all-inclusive, all-gay or all-lesbian Club Med packages; see the chapter "The Resort Experience" for details.

Another way to see the Caribbean is to take advantage of the many gay and lesbian cruises that are available. Travelers unfamiliar with the Caribbean sometimes prefer cruises because they get to visit several islands and decide where they'd like to return again for a land vacation. Others argue, however, that you can't really know what an island is like after a quick two-hour shore excursion. You'll have to decide for yourself—see the chapter on cruises for details and listings.

The Romantic Caribbean Getaway

Waves lap against white sand. Palm trees sway gently in a soothing breeze. The sun kisses your face as you lie back and sip a giant, fruity drink. You've never felt so rested, and you've never spent so much quality time with your lover.

There are several small, gay-friendly resorts eager to be the site of your next romantic getaway. Just ask Maddie Moynes, a Toronto resident who vacationed with her girlfriend at **Tingalayas,** an intimate bed and breakfast in out-of-the-way Negril, Jamaica. "I've been to Key West, Fort Lauderdale, and Provincetown," she says. "Personally, I prefer Negril. It depends on what you're looking for. If you want to cruise the bars, you want Fort Lauderdale. But if you want to get away on your own with a lover or a group of friends, Negril is great."

Tingalayas, which was started by a bisexual female artist from Canada, is part of a growing number of properties in smaller locations that market themselves to both straight and gay travelers. They allow lesbian and gay travelers the opportunity to visit places that are not large or liberal enough to support their own exclusively gay tourism industry.

The tiny property, which is the creation of a self-described "eccentric Canadian artist," features four terra-cotta, adobe-style cabanas that circle a central garden and a large, open kitchen—recreating a "primitive African village." A rock pool is a short walk away. Maddie and her girlfriend traveled throughout the town of Negril on bicycles, enjoying the natural beauty of the region, as well as local arts and crafts.

Negril, a small village located on the west coast of Jamaica, is known among straight tourists as an out-of-the-way, laid-back alternative to Jamaica's larger towns. But, like the rest of Jamaica, it's still not known as gay-friendly. So what about the safety issue? "You can go there and be comfortable," assures

Maddie. "I wouldn't hold hands in town, but you could say the same thing about parts of Toronto."

The Party-Hardy Caribbean Getaway

No other Caribbean island is better suited for gay nightlife than Puerto Rico. This island, a commonwealth of the United States, boasts more gay-oriented hotels, bars, businesses, and organizations than any other island in the Caribbean. "It's a fun environment," says Michael, who travels from his home in Kentucky at least once a year. "You've got your guest houses, which are very nice, and then at night, there's plenty of partying at the bars and discos."

Take note: While there are plenty of options (especially for gay men), Puerto Rico is still not West Hollywood or Boystown or Chelsea. You won't find as many gay pride flags flying, and you won't find huge industrial-sized gay discos, either. The fun of a place like Puerto Rico is that it is different, yet comfortable.

Gay bars and discos are similar to their counterparts in the United States, but don't expect the equivalent of a big Los Angeles nightclub—rather, appreciate the smaller venues and the friendly people.

Gay life is centered around the metropolitan San Juan area, which is divided into several neighborhoods. Ocean Park is where most of the gay and gay-friendly guesthouses are situated. They are generally comfortable, close to the beach, and offer discounts during the off-season (which is the summer and early fall—but don't even think about a trip here in the off-season if you hate the heat, or if there are hurricane warnings).

The largest gay hotel is the **Atlantic Beach Hotel,** located in the heart of the Condado district of Santurce, near many of the large tourist hotels and casinos. You can spend the early evening relaxing at the Atlantic Beach's beachfront bar, then head out bar-hopping. Condado is home to most of the gay bars in the region . . . although they're not necessarily the island's best. A few minutes' walk will bring you to Eros, the most popular gay and lesbian disco.

A super-stylish newcomer to the lodging market in the San Juan area is the **Water Club**, which is billed as Puerto Rico's first boutique hotel on the beach. While not exclusively gay, it is certainly gay friendly, and the property's unique style (something like a highly stylized Miami Beach establishment) and outstanding service certainly make it worth a stay, if its price fits into your budget. The Water Club is located in Isla Verde, the same neighborhood as San Juan's airport and a large number of upscale properties like the Ritz-Carlton and the El San Juan Hotel and Casino. But the Water Club stands out because of its trendy style, with dramatic lighting, waterfalls in the elevators (you have to see it to understand it), and bars that attract young, fashionable locals and visitors.

Even if you've come to Puerto Rico for sun and clubbing, don't forget about the many cultural attractions that make this island special.

In addition to the beaches (the gay sections are in front of the Atlantic Beach and in Ocean Park), Old San Juan is a must-see. This historic district, isolated from the rest of the city, has been beautifully preserved and, while a bit too commercial in some areas, has many historic churches, military buildings, and El Morro, a large fort used to protect the island in the days of Spanish rule.

If you have access to a car, plan at least two days to explore the rest of the island. Once you leave the San Juan area, you'll find a more genuine Puerto Rico filled with natural beauty and Spanish-style towns and cities—each one with its own town square, in true colonial style.

Less than an hour away from San Juan is El Yunque, the only tropical rain forest in our national park system. To the south, the city of Ponce offers historic architecture, an art museum, and a gay bar that serves the southwest region (there are other gay nightspots elsewhere on the island, too). San Germán, the second oldest city in Puerto Rico, boasts gorgeous Spanish colonial buildings, as well as a tiny gay bar, complete with pool table.

THINGS TO THINK ABOUT FIRST   What activities are you looking for—water sports, nightlife, quiet times on the beach, hiking, cultural festivals? What time of year are you traveling?

QUESTIONS TO ASK THE TRAVEL PROVIDER Are any meals included with the daily rate? Are any special discounts available? Do rooms have private baths? How far is the property from the beach/town/nightlife? How do I get there from the airport?

Recommended Accommodations

The following are small inns, hotels, and resorts in the Caribbean that welcome gay and lesbian travelers. Note: prices listed are in-season/off-season. In the Caribbean, in-season is generally between December and April; off-season is the rest of the year. Prices may fluctuate from year to year, but these listings will give you an idea of the price range. This is by no means an exhaustive listing, so consult your travel agent or gay destination guides for more information.

British Virgin Islands

The British Virgin Islands are not intensely developed in the commercial sense like some Caribbean destinations—but they still offer some gay-friendly establishments and ample access to the natural beauty of the region. The islands are a favorite for nature and beach enthusiasts, divers and snorkelers, and boating nuts.

Officially, about forty islands make up the British Virgin Islands. The largest are Virgin Gorda, Tortola, and Jost Van Dyke. Tortola features the highest mountain in the Virgin Islands, in Sage Mountain Park, as well as two top beaches: Cane Garden Bay and Apple Bay.

Among the attractions in Virgin Gorda are the Baths, a grouping of massive, ancient rocks that form watery nooks and crannies to explore. Off the coast of Salt Island, the wreck of the *R.M.S. Rhone,* an 1807 steam-powered ship, is one of the most popular dive sites in the Caribbean.

The Villas at Ft. Recovery PO Box 239, Tortola, BVI; 284-495-4354 (gay-friendly, 17 rooms, $145–$710). Accommodations are available with from one to four bedrooms. Full amenities, plus kitchens, living rooms, sun patio. The property features a pool, restaurant.

Jamaica

Tingalayas Bed & Breakfast Negril, Jamaica; 416-924-4269 (Toronto office), www.tingalayas.com (gay-friendly, $65, minimum four-night stay). This property is located in a rural area of Negril. The property is divided into two units. Unit A features two adjoining rooms, each with a double bed, ceiling fan, and a private bathroom. Unit B is the same, except each room has a loft with an additional double bed. Rooms can be rented individually, or you can take a whole unit.

Puerto Rico

Atlantic Beach Hotel 1 Calle Vendig, Condado/San Juan, PR 00907; 787-721-6900 (gay/lesbian, 37 rooms, $70–$150). This beachfront hotel hosts an active bar and features full amenities plus roof deck, Jacuzzi, and complimentary continental breakfast.

Embassy Guest House 1125 Seaview St., San Juan, PR 00907; 787-725-8284 (gay/straight, 12 rooms $65–$115/$45–$85, 1 suite $120–$145/$110). Full amenities, plus refrigerator, coffee maker, ceiling fans, and air-conditioning. Some rooms have kitchenettes.

Número Uno Guest House 1 Calle Santa Ana, San Juan, PR 00911; 787-726-5010 (gay/straight, $80–$245). This guest house, located in Ocean Park, is on the beach and features a pool and rooms with air-conditioning. Breakfast, lunch, and dinner are available on the premises.

Ocean Park Beach Inn Calle Elena, #3, San Juan, PR 00911; 787-728-7418 (lesbian/gay bed and breakfast; 10 rooms, $45–$115). Located in Ocean Park, this guest house features a sun deck and air-conditioned rooms with refrigerators. Some rooms have private baths, wet bars, kitchenettes. The restaurant and bar on the premises serves meals and refreshments.

Ocean Walk Guest House Atlantic Place, #1, Ocean Park/ San Juan, PR 00911; 787-728-0855 (lesbian/gay guest house, 40 rooms, 5 apts. $45–$140). A larger property in Ocean Park,

Ocean Walk is a complex of several buildings, joined by a court-yard and a pool. A small bar is also on the premises. Rooms feature TVs.

Water Club   2 Jose M. Tartak St., Isla Verde, PR 00979; 787-728-3666 or 888-265-6699 (lesbian and gay friendly, 84 rooms; $395). A trendy new entry into the San Juan hotel market, the plush Water Club features full amenities, a rooftop pool, fitness center, Sky Bar, restaurant, and a unique ambiance a few steps from the beach.

U.S. Virgin Islands

For years, the U.S. Virgin Islands were made up of three main islands: St. Thomas, St. John, and St. Croix. But in 1996, a fourth was added: Water Island, the site of a World War II military installation. If nothing else, this displays the region's U.S.-style know-how when it comes to getting additional publicity.

The tourism industry is equally well developed, with a wide range of hotel options and a relatively large selection of gay-friendly establishments—but you have to leave the larger towns if you want to experience the true beauty of the islands. Virgin Islands National Park, in St. John, boasts over nine thousand acres of protected wildlife and historical sites.

The largest island, St. Croix, is home to two towns with gingerbread-laced colonial Danish architecture, as well as Cormorant Beach and Sandy Point, the biggest beach of the islands.

The area around Charlotte Amalie, on St. Thomas, is where many accommodations are located, as well as extensive shopping opportunities (with cruise passengers invading regularly for shopping sprees). Here, you'll find several establishments ready to welcome gay and lesbian travelers.

Blackbeard's Castle   P.O. Box 6041, St. Thomas, USVI 00804; 800-344-5771 or 340-776-1234, www.blackbeardscastle.com (gay-friendly; 24 rooms, $135–$235). Located at the top of Black-beard's Hill, this historic landmark overlooks the town of

Charlotte Amalie. Rooms, which run from standard to junior suites and apartment suites, include full amenities, although some share bathrooms. On the premises is a pool, sun deck, and a bar with live performances.

Cormorant Beach Club & Hotel   4126 La Grande Princesse, St. Croix, USVI 00820; 800-548-4460 or 340-778-8920, www. cormorantbeachclub.com (gay and lesbian, $130–$265). This gay resort, large by local standards, features hotel rooms as well as a two-bedroom, 2.5-bath condo, and two beach studios. All rooms have a double sink vanity, air conditioning, ceiling fans, in-room safe, free local calls, cable television, CD clock radio and coffee maker, while the larger facilities have additional amenities such as kitchenettes. The resort also has tennis courts, massage services, a freshwater swimming pool, and bar.

Danish Chalet Guest House   P.O. Box 4319, St. Thomas, USVI 00803; 800-635-1531 or 340-774-5764. www.danishchaletinn. com (gay/straight, 12 rooms, $68–$99 including continental breakfast). This guest house also overlooks Charlotte Amalie, and rooms feature full amenities (except for some that don't have TV). The property also features a Jacuzzi spa and sun deck, plus an on-site bar offering $1 drink specials.

Hotel 1829   P.O. 1567, St. Thomas, USVI 00804; 800-524-2002 or 809-776-1829 (gay/straight, 15 rooms; suite with harbor view $220/$160; deluxe harbor view $180/$135; superior $135/$105; moderate $100/$75). This hotel features full amenities and a pool.

Pavilions & Pools Hotel   6400 Estate Smith Bay, St. Thomas, USVI 00802; 800-524-2001 or 340-775-6110, www.pavilionsand pools.com (gay/straight, 25 villas, $250–$275/$180–$195). True to its name, Pavilions & Pools is a collection of one-bedroom villas, each with its own private swimming pool. Villas have full amenities plus VCRs, kitchens with refrigerators, and ceiling fans. Some baths are shared, but all feature hair dryers. The property also has available a library, videos, massage services, plus snorkel gear and beach towels. Fishpond Terrace is the small bar located on the premises.

Saba

Tiny Saba, which measures only five square miles, is a tropical jewel built on an extinct volcano. The island can't compete with the beaches of neighboring Caribbean islands, but makes up for it with its underwater beauty in the Saba Marine Park, which surrounds the island. Featured in the park is a zone for snorkeling, swimming, diving, boating, and fishing, with ample opportunity to enjoy the splendor of the coral reef and underwater mountains.

Back on land, you can enjoy hiking, tours of the unique ecosystem of the island, and the culture of this member of the Dutch Windward island chain.

Queen's Gardens Resort   Troy Hill Drive 1, Saba, Netherlands Antilles; 159-946-3495 (gay-friendly, 12 units, $210–$1,500). This small hotel is made up of one- and two-bedroom suites that feature living area, bedrooms with ceiling fans or air conditioning, fully equipped kitchen, cable TV and telephone.

St. Barts

The chances you've already visited St. Barts is greatest if you happen to be wealthy or a celebrity. This small island in the French Caribbean has long been a preferred haunt of those in the so-called jet set. Today, there's a slightly broader base of tourism on the island, but you should still be on the lookout for the rich and famous.

St. Barts—or St. Barthélemy, as it's officially known—offers more than a dozen white sand beaches, the most popular of which is St. Jean. The island's capital, Gustavia, is a picturesque, relaxing town to visit.

Guanahani   Grand Cul de Sac, 97133 St. Barthélemy, French West Indies; 800-223-6800 or 011-590-27-6660, www.st-barths. com/guanahani-hotel/index.html (gay-friendly, 89 rooms, $290–$1650). This luxury property has 28 suites, 14 of which have their own pool (which explains the high room rates at the upper end). Facilities also include two restaurants, a confer-

ence room, a beauty salon, a boutique and plenty of opportunities for enjoying the great outdoors, including windsurfing,
snorkeling, tennis, and jet skis.

Caribbean-Wide

McLaughlin Anderson Vacations 100 Blackbeard's Hill
Suite 3, St. Thomas, U.S. Virgin Islands 00802; 800-537-6246 or
340-776-0635, www.mclaughlinanderson.com.
Offers homestays and apartment shares on several Caribbean
Islands: St. Thomas, St. John, St. Croix, Tortola, Virgin Gorda,
and Grenada. Accommodations range from hilltop estates to
seaside homes, some with private pools.

Resources

Alyson Adventures, 800-825-9766, www.alysonadventures.com
Amigos Tours, 800-881-7090 or 212-375-1100, www.amigos
tours.com
Atlantis Events, 800-628-5268, www.atlantisevents.com
Olivia Cruises and Resorts, 800-631-6277, www.olivia.com

Eye on Asia

There was a time when Asia was like another world for most
Americans. The cultures and standards in some Asian destinations were so far removed from our own that culture shock was
an inevitable and exciting part of the trip. But getting there
required great time and expense, placing it well out of the reach
of most vacationers.

Today, take a look around the Northwest Airlines wing at
Tokyo's Narita Airport, and you'll see nearly as many straight
American couples in matching jogging suits as you would in
Charlotte, North Carolina.

Visit some of the nations that make up this diverse region,
and you'll find signs of American popular culture, mixed in
strange and interesting ways with local flavor. (During a visit
to Bangkok, I found it impossible not to try McDonalds' "Samu-
rai Pork Burger.") But this encroaching Americanism isn't what

brings a growing number of visitors across the Pacific every year. It's the fascinating cultures, languages, and traditions that make each trip a challenging and stimulating experience. Organized gay and lesbian society exists in varying degrees across Asia. Some destinations, notably Bangkok and Manila, have reputations that precede them, based on reports of so-called "sex tourism." These cities do have more of the nightlife that gay men experience in the States, but they also have much more to offer than a few bars and hustlers. Cities like Hong Kong and Tokyo also offer some gay nightlife, as well as growing political organizations. The Hong Kong Tourist Association has begun its first efforts to promote gay and lesbian tourism. Singapore, a modern city by some measures, has a gay subculture that is harder to trace, while less-developed nations have yet to develop prominent lesbian and gay organizations or businesses.

Most gay and lesbian visitors focus on cultural and historic sights more than nonstop partying during their Asian expeditions. Escorted tours are an easy way to take in a lot of Asia in a little time (they can also be reassuring if you're intimidated by trying to read signs in a foreign alphabet).

Several companies offer tours.

If you really want to get some exercise, **Himalayan High Treks** helps visitors explore Nepal, India, Tibet, and Bhutan, on foot. **David Tours** offers an India tour that includes visits to New Delhi, Rajasthan, and Mumbai (Bombay), as well as two wildlife sanctuaries. Participants on this trip get to see such notable sites as the Taj Mahal, the Prince of Wales Museum, the Hanging Gardens in Mumbai, and the former Summer Palace of the Maharana of Udaipur.

Hanns Ebensten Travel offers a "China Redux" itinerary that includes visits to Beijing's Forbidden City and the Great Wall, followed by a flight south to the sacred mountains of Huangshan, to reach a hotel by cable car for the night. Next is an overnight train ride to Sun Yat-Sen's capital of Nanjing, Suzhou, and the Grand Canal. The journey concludes in Shanghai, staying at the well-known Peace Hotel and boarding a half-day cruise on the Yangtze River.

TRAVEL TIP

Tips for Charming the Pants off the Locals

(. . . or maybe just to make a good impression, even if
pants-removing is not on your itinerary.)

We people from the United States have a reputation abroad
for being rather ethnocentric. I, of course, always thought of
myself as Mr. World Traveler, far above the ignorant masses,
until one night in Toronto, when I stood, horrified, in a gay
bar, realizing I didn't know the name of Canada's prime minister (something like 90 percent of Canadians, on the other
hand, can name the U.S. president). In a matter of minutes, I
had lived up to the American stereotype, while disappointing
my Canadian friends, and perhaps ruining my chances with
one particularly cute guy at the bar.

You can avoid my mistake. Think before you travel, and
you'll get more out of your next trip. Here are some tips:

Learn something about the country before arriving. Do some
research, read some books and magazines, and talk to some
people who've been there. Can you name the current president, prime minister, or benevolent dictator?

Appreciate the differences of other cultures (even if that
means gritting your teeth while you're eating something
unidentifiable and disgusting). Remember, you're a guest in
their country. Don't expect it to be like home. Enjoy the differences, because that's what makes travel exciting.

Try to speak the language. Even if only a little bit. It will
work wonders in terms of showing people you respect their
culture, and prove that not all Americans are big fat ethnocentric pigs.

Respect the customs. In Thailand, you should never point
your foot at anyone while seated, nor should you pat
anyone—even children—on the head. Actions that mean nothing in our country can be very offensive in other parts of the
world (and vice versa, as you may have discovered while
watching a foreign visitor pick their nose in public here in the
United States).

Be sensitive to cultural differences. A gay lifestyle simply
doesn't exist in many countries, even though homosexual
activity is rampant. Don't try to convince an Egyptian that
they should be an exact duplicate of a North American gay-
rights activist.

* * *

When you display even a little knowledge about the place
you're visiting, locals will often warm up to you faster,
because they see you're really interested in their culture. It's
amazing what a little cultural awareness can do.

Other tour operators in the region include **Utopia Tours**,
a Bangkok-based company that offers packages to Thailand,
Vietnam, Cambodia, Laos, Bali, and Java. The company can
arrange customized itineraries for any arrival date, based on
travelers' interests. Complete travel plans can be made through
their Web site before arrival.

As tourism to Asia continues to grow, more tour options will
undoubtedly become available (there'll probably be even more
American fast food, too).

Resources

    David Tours, 888-723-0699, www.davidtours.com
    Hanns Ebensten Travel, 305-294-8174 or 866-294-8174, www.
hetravel.com
    Himalayan High Treks, 800-455-8735, www.himalayanhigh
treks.com
    Utopia Tours, 011-66-2-238-3227, www.utopia-tours.com

3

CRUISES

"One does not discover new lands without consenting to lose sight of the shore for a very long time."

—André Gide

Everyone has preconceived notions about what a cruise vacation is like. Some people think of it as a dream vacation, or a big party boat. A cruise may conjure up images of cruise director Julie's saccharin smile on *The Love Boat* or Shelley Winters' underwater heroics in *The Poseidon Adventure*.

Like these two actresses, cruises come in radically different shapes and sizes. You could spend several weeks luxuriating on a mighty ocean liner, or take a quick weekend scampering about in a spiffy little sail-powered craft. Destinations vary, too, from the far reaches of Asia to the nearer Caribbean. So do prices, which range from a few hundred to several thousand dollars.

Regardless of these variables, cruises offer benefits that keep people coming back for more. There's the convenience factor:

Since the trip is arranged and paid for in advance, there's very little left to worry about; you only have to unpack once; and on many ships, all on-board expenses are taken care of. All you have to do is relax and go with the flow.

If you're not sure that cruising is for you, "a cruise to nowhere" may help you decide. These cruises leave from major ports around the country and usually offer a one- or two-night package at a reasonable rate. Another option would be to take a short cruise to a nearby destination. **Pied Piper Travel**, which specializes in gay trips on upscale mainstream ships, offers relatively short itineraries to places like Bermuda, New England, and Canada.

Another option for travelers who are curious but uncertain about cruises is to take a tour that incorporates a cruise with a land tour, giving you the best of both worlds. The many islands of Greece, for example, make that nation an ideal setting for the combination land-and-sea vacations offered by several gay tour operators.

Once you've decided to take a cruise, there are several more things you'll have to decide:

The type of cruise. You have a choice when it comes to the kind of people you're going to cruise with. Mainstream cruises offer a wider variety of product, and you can sometimes go as part of a gay group. Cruises that are exclusively gay and/or lesbian, meanwhile, offer a shipwide sense of community and comfort rarely experienced anywhere else, plus itineraries designed especially for people like us.

The type of ship. Both gay and mainstream cruise packages offer choice in terms of the kind of ship you'll be on. The larger, more luxurious ships include the *QE2*, which usually plies the waters of the northeast and north Atlantic. Pied Piper Travel specializes in gay groups on this stately liner, providing separate group activities on board.

Gay vacationers looking for a more informal adventure may opt for a cruise on a windjammer, which is a smaller sailing ship with auxiliary power (the auxiliary motors kick in when there isn't enough wind). Windjammer cruises follow a leisurely itinerary, often touching shore at several Caribbean islands, with plenty of opportunity to kick your shoes off.

On a smaller scale, you could even charter a small yacht for a quick cruise offshore during a visit to one of your favorite destinations.

When and where to go. The time of year will influence where you go. Winter is the most popular time for a Caribbean cruise; fall or spring is a good time to visit the Mediterranean; and Alaska is beautiful in the summer. Some cruises only operate during certain times of year, while others are cheaper during the off-season.

The destinations you want to visit should take into account the activities you enjoy most, whether they be sunbathing, museum-hopping, shopping, sight-seeing, or swimming.

Price levels. Larger ships have the largest variety of price levels. Generally, the higher the stateroom is from the water, the more expensive it is. Rooms with a view are more expensive than those on the inside of the ship. The rooms vary in layout, too. Some have two single beds, some have a double, some are outfitted with multiple beds and hideaways to sleep several people. Before you decide on accommodations, you should ask to see a layout of the ship, to make sure you get what you want.

To get the best rates, making plans far in advance is usually a good idea—particularly for the gay cruises, which tend to have few departure dates available. Planning several months to a year in advance is recommended. For mainstream cruises, however, you can sometimes pick up a good sale with just a few weeks' notice. To help cut costs, be as flexible as you can with your travel dates and ask your travel agent about any new ships or routes that might be offering lower fares. Discounts may be offered for a second person in your cabin, as well. In addition, you can sometimes have airfare included in the price of your cruise. Airfare is usually an add-on, so the tour company or your travel agent should help you find the lowest possible airfare to the point of embarkation (i.e., the port from which the ship sails).

When calculating how much a cruise will cost, be sure you know exactly what will be included. The price of your ticket may not include drinks, tips, and shore excursions—in fact, most cruise companies make the bulk of their profits from shore excursions, casinos, duty-free purchases, and other optional add-ons. You should ask how much these additional amenities will cost, and in the case of shore excursions, ask whether the cost covers a guided tour or just transportation to the shore.

Cruise lines and tour companies have come up with some interesting special-interest tours—both gay and mainstream. You can enjoy a music festival, sail with members of a sports team, or attend a spiritual retreat, all without touching ground. Some cruises tie in with special landbound events, such as **RSVP's** Mardi Gras cruise, which offers the opportunity to celebrate New Orleans' famed holiday from a home base of RSVP's chartered 1,214-passenger ship. After a day of joining in the festivities in the French quarter, passengers return to their home ship for RSVP's own special costume party.

THINGS TO THINK ABOUT FIRST   What level of luxury do you want and what can you afford? What time of year will you be traveling? Do you feel more comfortable on an all-gay cruise or traveling on a mainstream ship? What are your personal interests? What kind of land vacations do you usually take? What type of itinerary do you want? Would you rather spend several days in a couple of ports of call, or hit a bunch of destinations for brief visits? What activities do you enjoy—shopping, sightseeing, water sports?

QUESTIONS TO ASK THE TRAVEL PROVIDER   What is included in the package? Can I see a layout of the ship? What types of cabins are available, and what is the price range? What itineraries are available? What activities are available on board and at the ports of call? What kinds of people usually travel on the cruise? What exactly does the price include—meals, drinks, activities, entertainment, escorted shore excursions?

Mainstream Cruises

David Zeni and Jamie Watkins are big fans of mainstream cruises—especially aboard the legendary *QE2,* which they've sailed on several times.

"If you take a gay cruise," they warn, "it's a ragtag, motley bunch. They're people you really don't want to get to know." Granted, David and Jamie don't know this from firsthand experience; they've never done an all-gay cruise and have no desire to. They admit that this may be because they live in Province-town, a town sometimes overwhelmed by vacationing homo-sexuals. "It's different being on the *QE2*, because we're not inundated with gay people."

Sailing mainstream still requires a certain amount of caution. For example, Jamie points out, "Carnival tends to attract the more heterosexual, younger crowd." When the couple sailed on ships that were less expensive than the *QE2*, "they all had sort of 'Ma and Pa Kettle' types, people on their first cruise. I remember once Jamie was wearing a very tasteful earring at dinner, and I saw a lady from Iowa pointing at it. You don't get that on the *QE2*."

With the more pricey *QE2* cruise, "you're traveling with a more sophisticated group of people. People take it seriously. They tend to dress up for dinner. It's sort of a classy, festive kind of thing. It's like having glamour put back in your life. It's the closest thing you can get to doing it the way they used to do it."

"The service is incredible," David continues. "You can ask for just about anything and get it. They can't do enough for you." As with just about everything in life, you get what you pay for.

Don't think that just because you're on a mainstream ship that you're all alone. "A large number of the crew are gay," David and Jamie say, and if they realize you're gay, "they have little red flags that go up, and they take better care of you than they do the others. They go out of their way for you."

David and Jamie arrange most of their cruises through **Pied Piper,** a tour operator that books groups of gay people on board mainstream ships. "One of the advantages of booking with Pied Piper is that you can book a mainstream cruise and know there'll be other gay people on board," Jamie says.

Pied Piper reserves cabins for its clients throughout the ship, but it arranges for the gay groups to dine together.

Included in most of the Pied Piper cruises is a welcome-aboard cocktail party, an on-board Pied Piper tour escort, a private tour of the ship, a cocktail and welcome party with the captain, a midnight pool party (weather permitting), meals and entertainment, a group photo, and arranged visits and parties with the local gay community at some ports, as well as optional private escorted shore excursions.

The *QE2*'s most popular sailing is across the Atlantic, but there are additional opportunities to enjoy this grande dame while visiting other destinations. Past Pied Piper offerings have included a Rio-to-New York journey that included a two-night precruise land package in Rio. A five-day cruise to Bermuda featured socializing with the local gay community on the island.

The *QE2*'s six-day European shopping cruise sails from Southampton, England, to ports in Germany, the Netherlands, Belgium, and France. At cities like Hamburg, Amsterdam, Zeebrugge, and LeHavre, passengers shop for fashions, artwork, leather goods, perfumes, and a host of other goodies.

Music fans appreciate the Newport Jazz Festival Cruise, during which the *QE2* spends six days meandering between New York City and Newport, Rhode Island, where renowned jazz musicians keep things lively on board.

A similar route is followed during the *QE2* New England/ Canada Fall Foliage Cruise, which provides views of the many colors of the season, as well as stops at Portland and Bar Harbor, Maine, St. John, New Brunswick, and Newport, Rhode Island.

Sometimes, gay groups can actually turn the ship gay, at least a little bit. One night, David and Jamie remember, "there were sixteen of us sitting in the club [on board the ship]. We ended up getting up and dancing together, and nobody said a word."

Pied Piper offers vacation packages aboard other upscale mainstream ships, as well. Examples include a cruise through the Baltic sea aboard the **Crystal Symphony,** departing from Copenhagen, Denmark, and making stops in places like Helsinki, St. Petersburg, Stockholm, and Oslo on its way to London.

Their seven-day Alaska cruise, aboard one of Cunard's newest ocean liners, visits Skagway, Juneau, Wrangell, Ketchikan, and the Hubbard Glacier, taking in the breathtaking beauty of our biggest state.

For all the Pied Piper cruises departing from New York, the company also makes available (for an additional charge) a two-night New York City hotel and sight-seeing package that includes accommodations, a tour, transfers to the hotel and ship, and the services of a local Pied Piper representative.

Pied Piper regularly offers a variety of itineraries, including a 14-day "Carnaval in Rio" cruise, which departs from Buenos Aires and stops in Uruguay and Brazil, just in time for three days of Carnaval.

Ocean Voyager is another company that offers gay group tours aboard mainstream ships. Their packages have used the ships of several companies, including Princess Cruises, the Holland America Line, Majesty Cruise Line, Celebrity Cruises, and Royal Caribbean. Destinations aboard Ocean Voyager cruises have included Alaska, the Mediterranean, the Caribbean, Mexico, and Hawaii.

Ocean Voyager's Thanksgiving Cruise aboard the 77,000-ton *Sun Princess* was a seven-night excursion from Fort Lauderdale, with stops in the Bahamas, Jamaica, Grand Cayman, and Mexico's Yucatan Peninsula. The massive ship, which boasts over 400 staterooms and suites with private balconies, features five restaurants, including a pizzeria, patisserie, twenty-four-hour food court, and two intimate dining rooms. Passengers can stay in shape in spite of overeating, thanks to a glass-enclosed fitness center, which surrounds a pool that is suspended between two decks.

Entertainment on the *Sun Princess* includes performances in a theater and show lounge/cabaret. And traveling with Ocean Voyager's gay group means there are some extras: a "welcome aboard" cocktail party for gay passengers, the services of an Ocean Voyager host, special nautical souvenirs, prearranged group dining, and a group beach party. Add-on packages for a stay in Fort Lauderdale or Miami Beach are always a great way to round out any cruise from South Florida.

Additional cruises with Ocean Voyager have featured Presidents' Day and Valentine's Day on a Royal Majesty cruise to Key West and Nassau, a Celebrity Cruises trip to the eastern Caribbean, and a beach-hopping Caribbean voyage on Royal Caribbean's new ship, *Grandeur of the Seas*. *Grandeur* boasts a seven-deck-high atrium, indoor and outdoor swimming pools, a health spa, and Broadway-style theater.

One final note about mainstream cruises: If you're a male over age fifty, you may be able to travel for free. How? By signing on as a "gentleman host." You have to be willing to dine, dance, and mingle with heterosexual female passengers—mainstream cruise lines like to provide company for single older women. Don't worry, intimate relations are not part of the job. If you think you can handle it, contact the host program division of the cruise line that interests you.

Resources

Ocean Voyager, 800-435-2531, www.oceanvoyager.com
Pied Piper Tours, 800-TRIP-312, www.gaygroupcruises.com

Gay Men's Cruises

When an **RSVP** cruise sets sail, you'll usually find an awful lot of happy homosexuals on board. This ain't no Love Boat, this is 47,000 tons of gay fun.

What's the difference between a gay and a mainstream cruise? "It's like living in Chelsea versus living in the projects," says David Lammerding, referring to the openness that characterizes New York City's gayest neighborhood. David has taken several mainstream cruises too, and admits there are advantages to both (there are obviously a lot more mainstream cruises available, so there's a lot more to choose from).

But the decision is yours. David suggests you ask yourself a few questions: "Would you rather be on a boat where all your neighbors and everyone is gay? If you want to hold hands with your lover on the deck, go RSVP." Plus, he says, "single guys can get laid easier on gay cruises, unless you go for the staff or the entertainment on a mainstream cruise."

Aside from hand-holding and easier pickings, gay cruises can offer the quality and scope of a mainstream cruise, on some of the most comfortable ships afloat. Like most gay and lesbian cruises, RSVP charters entire ships from mainstream lines— something that was not easy to arrange when the company started out in the 1980s. "Ten years ago, most major cruise lines didn't want to be associated with gay groups," David says. "Now everybody's heard that RSVP does a great job and it actually helps the cruise line, so a lot of the lines have changed." Now, David points out, more gay cruises are aboard some of the best ships afloat.

Gay cruises offer a wide variety of itineraries—almost as many as mainstream cruises—at a variety of prices, based on where you're going and the type of cabin you want (obviously, the larger ones with beautiful views from the upper levels fetch the higher prices). David says that Atlantis and RSVP in particular offer good value.

RSVP offers several cruises to destinations in the Caribbean, Mexico, and Europe. The company's Los Angeles-Mexico cruise takes place aboard Carnival Cruise Line's MS Ecstasy. The ship features complimentary room service, a 24-hour pizzeria, a coffee and pastry bar, three swimming pools (one with a waterslide), a two-story show room, a five-story grand atrium, a salon and gym, a spa, a running track, and great deck space to enjoy the sun, pool games, and afternoon tea dances. Oh, and there are 15 bars and lounges, too. The 10-day cruise makes stops at San Diego, Manzanillo, Puerto Vallarta, Mazatlan, and Cabo San Lucas. Past RSVP cruises have featured name-brand on-board entertainment such as Nell Carter, Sandra Bernhard, and Jimmy James. During port calls, travelers can shop, go horseback riding, water ski, or parasail—or just chill on the beach. On board, activities both day and night keep the mood festive.

Other offerings from RSVP have included a cruise of the eastern Mediterranean, which featured visits to the Greek islands and Turkish mosques. RSVP's South American cruise set sail from Buenos Aires and visited Montevideo, Punta del Este, and

Florianópolis—home of forty-two different beaches—on its way to gay hot spot Rio de Janeiro. A northern European cruise began in Tilbury, England, stopping in Hamburg, Amsterdam, Zeebrugge, and St. Malo on its way to Le Havre, France, with plenty of time to explore each stop. In 1995, RSVP opened their cruises to women, although the majority of their passengers are still men. Read on for more women's options.

Cruises for gay men are available from many tour operators. Atlantis Events, which also allows women aboard, has been offering an annual Miami cruise for several years, most recently aboard the 1,950-passenger Norwegian Sun. The cruise features plenty of onboard activities, including nine restaurants, two swimming pools, a two-story theater, dance parties, volleyball and basketball court, eight bars and lounges, live music nightly and other live entertainment. The cruise makes stops at San Juan, St. Croix, Tortola, and Nassau. The company's Hawaiian Islands cruise is aboard the Norwegian Star, billed as the fourth largest passenger vessel in the world. The ship makes port calls at Honolulu, Kona, Fanning Island, Lanaina (Maui), and Nawiliwili (Kauai). In addition to plenty of amenities and activities similar to those on other Atlantis cruises, this one has some destination specific, including hula lessons, luaus, Hawaiian shows, and the opportunity to learn about Hawaiian culture and folklore.

Nubian Knight Tours, a Decatur, Georgia-based company, offers a number of men's tours aboard mainstream ships. While the tours are targeted at African-American men, all races are welcome. "We service the conservative crowd," the company's Web site explains, "especially those who are on the DL, laid back and are not into the traditional gay scene." Among the cruise destinations offered are the Bahamas, Puerto Rico, and New Orleans (for Mardi Gras).

Resources

Atlantis Events, 800-628-5268, www.atlantisevents.com
Nubian Knight Tours, 770-322-9535, www.blackgaymentours. com
RSVP Travel Productions, 800-328-RSVP, www.rsvp.net

Women's Cruises

"I've always been a traveler," says Mary Gay of Richmond, Virginia, "and I think cruising is the freest thing in the world. You get a sense of what the world would be like if it weren't homophobic." Mary took her first **Olivia** cruise in 1991 and has climbed aboard a cruise ship every year since then.

Olivia leases entire ships (and resorts, too, but that's another section) for its trips. They're for women only—and that's part of the attraction, Mary says. "Traveling with lesbians is an important thing," she explains. "And I always meet the nicest people. If you're single, it's a great way to meet women. I went single on four of the five cruises, and I don't think I ever sat out on a dance." If you're already coupled off, don't worry: there are plenty of couples on board, too.

On-board activities abound. "I've done everything," says Mary. "I've done the dating game. I've done the talent show. I've done a lip synch. It's the same kind of stuff you do on straight cruises, except it's more fun."

"Cruises appeal to a lot of people because you can do what you want to," Mary continues. "You can do real low-key activities or you can dance every dance. There's something there for everybody. They even do networking lunches so you can meet other people in your profession."

On-board entertainment also includes musicians and comedians. "The entertainment is always good," Mary reports. "And they get you involved, too. One of the peak moments of my life was two-stepping on deck when the sun was setting."

During her cruises, Mary has played golf on Caribbean islands during stopovers; she's also visited glaciers along the dramatic shores of the Alaskan coastline. "They do a good job preparing small Alaskan communities for a shipload of lesbians coming in," she adds. "You dump a thousand lesbians into a town and we own the town!"

As with most gay and lesbian cruises, the ships are straight-owned and vary in size and style. "They've all been really nice.

Some of them are grand, some are smaller," explained Mary. The straight crews have also been commendable, she added. "I've gotten to sit at the captain's table a couple times. And they always make a toast to human rights. The crew may have some preconceived ideas, but we've been treated perfectly by every captain, every waiter. I think this is the way we're going to change the world, by people seeing us in our normal environment."

Among the cruises offered by Olivia is a South Pacific voyage aboard one of Renaissance Cruises' new R-Class ships. The ships feature several options for dining and amenities like a casino, sports bar, fitness center, spa, and library. When passengers aren't sailboarding, waterskiing, snorkeling, or windsurfing, they may want to work out in the ship's gymnasium, take a dip in the pool or hot tub, or visit the piano bar and lounge. Entertainers heat up the night with comedy and song once the ship pushes off from its starting point in Tahiti.

The ship stops at several islands, including Moorea, Huahine, Raiatea, Bora Bora, and Tahiti, where passengers can scuba dive, surf, ride horseback, canoe, and bicycle—all against the backdrop of beautiful beaches and lush native flora and fauna.

Other women-only cruises are offered by a number of companies. **Women Sail Alaska,** which is written about in the section titled "Women Sail Alaska, Too," even offers the chance to sail and navigate. **Skylink's** itineraries include the United States, Europe, Hawaii, and Africa.

Airfare isn't usually included in lesbian cruise packages, and Mary admits that the trips are "a bit more expensive than other cruises, but it's well worth it. I've always said that Olivia could cruise in Detroit, and I'd go."

Resources

Olivia Cruises and Resorts, 800-631-6277, www.olivia.com
Skylink Women's Travel, 800-CALL-SKY, www.skylinktravel. com
Women Sail Alaska, 888-272-4525, www.alaska.net/~sailak/

It's Not the Size of the Ship, It's the Motion of the Ocean: Sailing on Smaller Ships

Sure, a big ship can carry thousands of fun-loving homosexuals to exotic ports of call, and offer them sparkling on-board discos and casinos for their nights at sea. But that's not what *everyone* wants from a seagoing experience. Smaller ships can get you closer to the sea in a more intimate setting.

Tom Bolton is an Atlanta-based sailing fan who's gone on several cruises with Windjammer Barefoot Cruises' all-gay charters. Windjammers are ships with sails where passengers can actually join in the sailing if they desire (auxiliary power kicks in if the wind is no good).

Tom's Yankee Clipper sailing adventure was aboard a sixty-four-passenger restored classic vessel, complete with mahogany fittings.

Tom says that smaller ships are pleasantly sociable. "It's kind of different than being on a big ship with two thousand people," Tom says. "You can really get to know the people. You go scuba diving with the guys. We even rented motorbikes.

"Usually, there are three levels of people on the trips," Tom explains. "There's the older people who have the money and come to enjoy it. Then there's the first-timers, who've heard about it from somebody; their average age is in the thirties. Then you've got a whole set of young people who want to check it out. The mix is excellent."

The smaller size also fosters a casual atmosphere that many people like. "It's very laid back, not formal. Everything is optional, so you can chart your own course. If you want to go scuba diving, you go scuba diving. Some people stay on the boat, some people go mountain climbing and see every tourist attraction. If we're having a Halloween party, some people just have a cocktail and enjoy watching other people."

For the Windjammer Barefoot Cruises, all meals are included, as well as accommodations. "From the time you get on, all your food and some activities are included."

One of the misconceptions about windjammer cruises, Tom says, is that passengers are *required* to hoist sails and work the decks every day. That's just not true, he says. You don't have to work at all, although you're welcome to get involved with the crew's activities if you want to.

Windjammer has also offered cruises on the larger *Star Clipper,* which boasts thirty-six thousand square feet of sails, two pools, a piano bar, and library.

Other players in the smaller-ship category include **RSVP,** well-known for its heavy ship excursions. RSVP offers several itineraries in the Mediterranean aboard the relatively small, 228-passenger Royal Clipper. Billed as "the largest true sailing ship in the world," the ship features several types of cabins, including a suite, a cabin with two twin beds, and a cabin with a small double bed. RSVP has used the Royal Clipper for itineraries calling in France, Italy, Greece, and Turkey.

Journeys By Sea specializes in gay yacht vacations across the globe, with the option of booking the entire ship or joining an existing itinerary (with your own stateroom, of course). Entire yachts can also be chartered with **Port Yacht Charters,** which specializes in the Caribbean, New England, and the Mediterranean. **Water Fantaseas,** based in Fort Lauderdale, Florida, charters a forty-four-foot private yacht for excursions in the region. In the Northeast, **Sailing Affairs** offers group charters and trips for individuals aboard a thirty-eight-foot sailboat, with cabins to sleep a total of six people. Itineraries vary by request, and generally cover the entire East Coast. Tall ship cruises have also been offered by **Men on Vacation.**

Resources

Journeys By Sea, 800-825-3682, www.journeysbysea.com
Men on Vacation, 888-333-4668, www.menonvacation.com
Nubian Knight Tours, 770-322-9535, www.blackgaymentours.com
Port Yacht Charters, 800-213-0465, www.portyachtcharters.com
RSVP, 800-328-RSVP, www.rsvp.net
Sailing Affairs, 212-228-5755
Water Fantaseas, 954-524-1234, www.waterfantaseas.com

Windjammer Barefoot Cruises, 800-2-GAY-CRUISE or 213-654-7700, www.gaywindjammer.com

Exploring Alaska

Luke Hallenbeck had heard a lot of good things about Alaska. "It's been on my priority list, right below Egypt," he says. "So I went to Egypt in January and said, 'This is the summer for Alaska.'"

He'd wanted to go to the far-off state for quite a while, and going on a gay tour, one which incorporated a cruise with land travel, seemed to be the perfect opportunity. He signed up for a twelve-day tour of Alaska and the Yukon. The tour explored a large chunk of the state and ended with a cruise aboard Holland America Line's *Nieuw Amsterdam* from Juneau, via Glacier Bay and the Inside Passage, to Vancouver.

The trip began with a flight from Seattle to Anchorage. From there, the group set forth on an eight-day land-based excursion. The first stop was a two-day visit in Denali National Park, a six-million acre reserve of tundra and glacial streams dominated by America's highest peak, the 20,320-foot Mount McKinley. Luke's group, which consisted of twenty-six people, learned more about the park's ecosystem and saw many of the natural wonders they'd heard about.

"We took a marvelous small boat and saw the Columbia Glacier, which was fabulously beautiful," Luke says. "We saw sea lions, we saw puffins, and sea otters. It was so beautiful, so unhurried, and the people driving the boat would get us as close as they could to everything." Next up was a cruise on the *Glacier Queen III* into Prince William Sound, past the enormous Columbia Glacier, and on to Valdez. The tour then took the Keystone Canyon road out of Valdez to join the Glenn Highway and the Alaska Highway into Beaver Creek, a gateway to the Yukon. Next was a stop at Whitehorse, Yukon headquarters of the Canadian Mounties.

A trip aboard the antique cars of the narrow-gauge White Pass & Yukon Railroad began just south of Whitehorse, for a scenic journey over White Pass to Skagway, followed by a cruise from Skagway to Juneau.

"Another highlight was when we took a helicopter trip and flew over the mountains to the Mendenhall glacier," Luke adds. "They have an observation post there. The people there were very gracious to us and I felt amazed that I was walking over so much ice." The three-night Inside Passage cruise swept through Glacier Bay National Park and docked at Sitka.

If it sounds like a jam-packed schedule, that's because it was. In general, there wasn't much free time on the tour because "the tour covered a tremendous amount of mileage," Luke explains. "That was one of the hardest things about the trip. Some days we'd be on the bus for twelve hours. But that's because of Alaska's size. When people look at it on the map, you don't realize that Alaska is four times the size of Texas."

Everything, including most meals, was included, from the time they got on the plane in Seattle until they got off the boat in Vancouver (all meals were included in the cruise portion of the trip).

Luke enjoyed the friendships established within his group. "I think one of the nicest things is that you all have the same mental attitude," he says, adding that most of the people in his group were in couples.

He now understands why tourism to Alaska has increased in recent years. "Twenty years ago, people didn't have the money to go," he says. "But now people see things about it, hear things about it, the magnitude of it." He says summer was the perfect time to visit the region. "The weather was delightful and the flowers were fabulous—vivid in colors that you couldn't believe," he recalls. "Every town we visited had hanging flowers."

Traveling to Alaska does involve a bit of adjustment. "At that time of year, there were very few hours of night—about three to four hours of dark," Luke says.

Obviously, Alaska is not for people looking for an urban vacation, although they did have some time to explore the towns along the route. "Alaska is redneck," Luke warns. "We were given the name of one bar. I think some of the fellows went there, but didn't think much of it. I asked on the Internet before I went if anyone knew any men in Alaska, and I got only one answer.

"There wasn't much sophistication as far as when we went into town," he adds. "We saw these little shows that they have in great big bars, and they were okay, but they'll never make Broadway."

That may be because even though the state is huge, the cities are not. "Anchorage is only about two hundred fifty thousand people. Juneau is tiny. But my favorite was Sitka; it was more like a real little town, with an old movie house downtown. It also has a tremendous Russian influence, and the beautiful little cathedral there was Russian Orthodox with icons that were hundreds of years old."

Several tour operators offer gay cruises to Alaska, including Atlantis Events, Pied Piper, Glacier Bay Tours, and Gay Cruise Vacations.com.

Resources

Atlantis Events, 800-628-5268, www.atlantisevents.com
Gay Cruise Vacations.com, 888-367-9398, www.gaycruise vacations.com
Glacier Bay Tours, 800-451-5952, www.glacierbaytours.com
Pied Piper Tours, 800-TRIP-312, www.gaygroupcruises.com

Women Sail Alaska, Too

The pleasures of sailing on a smaller ship are brought sharply into focus when we're talking about Alaska; it seems the closer you get to the region's natural beauty, the better. **Women Sail Alaska** provides female travelers with plenty of opportunities to see southeastern Alaska close up. The lesbian-guided charters, which serve groups limited to four people, allows for whale watching, photography, beach walking, birding, and fishing. The variety of wildlife is impressive, from hummingbirds and wrens to whales, sea lions, and seals.

TRAVEL TIP

Meet the People Who Make Vacations

Besides travel agents, books, and magazines, there are other ways you can keep up on the latest gay travel news. One of them is by meeting the people who make the vacations, and the best place to do that is at Gay and Lesbian Travel Workshops, which are held in several large cities throughout the United States every year, culminating in the Gay and Lesbian World Travel Expo.

The events are organized by Community Marketing, a San Francisco-based gay travel marketing organization. For a nominal fee, you can talk with people representing various tour companies, travel agencies, gay-popular destinations, and even airlines. Even though it's primarily for travel industry professionals, it can be a helpful way to get some new travel ideas and maybe even make some travel friends.

For information, call Community Marketing at 800-GAY-EXPO or 415-552-5140 or MARK8ING@aol.com or visit them at http://www.mark8ing.com.

Another source is the International Gay Travel Association, which can connect you with travel agents and tour operators. Call them at 800-448-8550 or visit them at http://www.iglta.org. The online site lists over 1,100 travel-related members.

Travelers interested in boating can learn sailing skills, boat handling, navigation, and anchoring, as well as the use of electronics and safety procedures.

Accommodations on board include a double berth forward, a double and single berth in the main saloon, and a quarter berth aft. A cabin heater keeps passengers warm and dry, and an on-board library provides diversion from the fantastic scenery.

Cuisine includes a variety of local catches, and all food and beverages are included on charters of more than half a day, although no alcohol is provided.

Theresa Tavel is a U.S. Coast Guard-licensed skipper. She and her partner Karen Walter have been sailing in southeast Alaska for more than fifteen years, and both have an affection for the region that they share with their passengers.

Several itineraries are available. The five- or six-day trip to Tracy Arm, an inlet south of Juneau, passes an array of wildlife and glaciers. A day trip up Tracy Arm ends at Sawyer Glacier, beneath sheer, three-thousand-foot granite cliffs.

The five- to seven-day trip down Stephens Passage sails around the tip of the Glass Peninsula on Admiralty Island, up into Seymour Canal. Tour organizers Walter and Tavel say that spotting a humpback whale is quite likely on this excursion.

The five- to seven-day trip down the west side of Admiralty Island takes passengers to Tenakee Springs, a small village with a hot springs and no automobiles—perfect for walking and hiking. Karen and Theresa recommend this trip during the Summer Solstice, when twenty hours of daylight allows visitors to watch the sun set and rise without going to sleep.

A couple of quicker, one-day trip options involve a visit to Taku Inlet, with towering mountain peaks and glaciers, or an abbreviated visit to Admiralty Island, watching for whales, seals, porpoises, and other wildlife.

Resources

Women Sail Alaska, 888-272-4525, www.alaska.net/~sailak/

4

SPECIAL INTEREST TOURS

"Travelers are often advised to take a long
book on their journeys, but who would
devote his attention to a book which will
always be at hand when he can turn the
dog-eared pages of a total stranger whom
he may never meet again?"

—Quentin Crisp

On your next vacation, you could explore your spirituality in
the Bahamas, wear leather chaps to an ancient German castle,
or celebrate with sissies by Cinderella's Castle.

Yes, gay and lesbian travel has gone beyond vanilla, main-
stream-style tours to encompass a wider range of interests.
It only makes sense: The lesbian and gay community is so
diverse, there's no way that standard gay travel packages could
satisfy everyone.

Travelers on these more focused tours usually share a
common interest or identity (beyond being gay or lesbian) that

is emphasized during the trip. We'll take a look at several in this chapter.

There are plenty of offbeat packages available besides these listed here, but because they tend to operate less frequently (or may only operate once), it's harder to keep track of what's being offered at any given time. We recommend you do your research.

Pete's Travel and Tours, based in San Francisco, offers tours and packages that are "bear-friendly," that is, geared toward large men (with a certain amount of body hair) and those who admire them. The company's diverse offerings include a Windjammer Barefoot Caribbean cruise charter, an excursion to Alaska, and Rancho Cicada, a clothing-optional resort in California.

Bear-friendly excursions are also available from **Ursa Travel** of Providence, RI. Ursa has offered a Caribbean cruise leaving from San Juan that featured stops at St. Lucia, Antigua, St. Maarten, St. Thomas, and St. Croix. Other trips include a trip to Amsterdam, a "Bear Group" to Gay Day at Disney, and a cruise to Alaska.

For women, there are plenty of opportunities for special-interest travel, too. **Rving Women**, for example, is a company specializing in events and trips for female enthusiasts of recreational vehicles. The company offers maintenance and driving classes, rallies, conventions, and parties throughout the year in various parts of the United States.

Carol Nashe Group, based in Boston, offers several women-only golf trips to several top destinations, as well as mainstream golf excursions.

Obviously, special interest tours serve a more limited market than most, so there's less product to choose from. But there are new tour products sprouting up every day, so keep in touch with your travel agent. In addition, special interest tours are sometimes conducted by political or social organizations (such as Act Up and the Names Project), rather than tour companies, so keep in touch with groups that interest you for news.

THINGS TO THINK ABOUT FIRST   What special interests or concerns do you have? Would you like to have them become a central part of your vacation? Would you like to meet other people with similar interests and concerns? Do you enjoy interacting on an emotional/spiritual level with other people? What kinds of trip activities are appropriate for you? Do you belong to any organizations where members might be interested in a particular kind of vacation or retreat?

QUESTIONS TO ASK THE TRAVEL PROVIDER   What sorts of activities are planned? Is there a leader, and if so, what is the leader's background? What is included in the cost (accommodations, meals, activities)? Are refunds guaranteed in case of cancellation?

Spiritual and Well-Being Tours

"The first **Spirit Journeys** trip I did literally changed my life," says Brian Zerr, a writer based in Boulder, Colorado. "It was just an amazing experience. I left there saying, 'I want every day of my life to be like this.' I walked away feeling very proud of who I was." He has since been on three trips with Spirit Journeys.

Brian had the unforgettable experience of swimming with dolphins during a catamaran excursion off the coast of Grand Bahama. But that wasn't what changed his life—it was his interaction with the other people on this spiritual retreat. "By the end of the week," he says, "I felt like I really cared about everyone on the boat."

That's one of the goals of these tours, which focus not only on outdoor activities, but on inner well-being and group interaction. Trips are available for men and women, usually separately, from various operators.

Spirit Journeys operates a variety of tours. "They're a really neat outfit, because they're trying not only to have a travel experience, but a bonding experience," says Joe, who recently traveled with the group to New Mexico.

Brian says that other gay vacations focus too much on sex and drinking, whereas a spiritually focused trip is more fulfilling in the long run. Each trip with Spirit Journeys features group discussions and guided exercises, during which guests are encouraged to share their feelings and experiences. This, Brian explains, helps to create intimacy and caring within the group. "You kind of learn how to live in a community. Other trips, and society in general, don't support that."

Joe concurs. "They have a focus throughout their trips of breaking barriers down between people and getting in touch with a spiritual aspect of yourself," he says, adding that "definitely this is not for everybody, but it attracts people who are looking for more than just a good time. I suspect the bonds that I formed there will be lasting."

What difference does it make if a spiritual retreat is gay? "Number one, you get to be boys. All the walls are down. There's a certain freedom traveling only with gay men."

Spirit Journey's groups are usually between ten and twenty-five men, and packages generally include lodging and food, in addition to other activities.

The Spirit Journey trips range from dolphin swimming in the Bahamas to a winter retreat in Mexico; from a couples' workshop in West Palm Beach to river rafting on Texas's Rio Grande. "The rafting and camping trips are more rugged," Brian advised.

In recent years, the company has increased the variety of international itineraries it offers. Its "Pilgrimage to the Sacred Andes of Peru" includes four days of exploring in the Cuzco area, five days in the Sacred Valley, three days at Machu Picchu, a healing ceremony (led by shamans) as well as special ceremonies and meditations throughout the trip. Their "Journey to Tibet and Nepal" includes meditation at a Buddhist monastery, visits to several sacred sites, boating on Phewa Lake, mountain hiking, and a visit to the oldest monastery in Tibet. Other packages are available to Costa Rica, Egypt, and Bali.

"If you're looking for a place to meet some real quality people, that's certainly what Spirit Journeys is about," says Brian. "It's not just a vacation. It's a place to get centered. You have the opportunity to connect with nature, connect with other men, and to learn more about yourself."

Hawk, I'm Your Sister, a Santa Fe-based tour operator, offers an extensive selection of trips for women, although they are not exclusively lesbian.

Many of Hawk's tours are canoe trips, and group members share a variety of daily tasks, from food preparation and cleanup to loading canoes and digging latrines.

The themes of Hawk's trips vary. A journey up Montana's Missouri River was the setting for a recent writing retreat. Writing was also the focus of a visit to Heron Lake, in New Mexico. In describing her company's offerings, Beverly Anteus of Hawk writes, "By attending equally to the inner and the natural worlds, we can find the common narrative flowing through these worlds and the web that interconnects them."

A Hawk group has also visited the Bahamas for an ocean workshop. "The purpose of this retreat/workshop is to establish ourselves as a community of women and reestablish our relationship and our response to the ocean," says Beverly. In other words, rather than simply exploring the water, the group explored their relationship to the water through swimming, snorkeling, scuba diving, sailing, and windsurfing—with time each day to gather together and share their feelings and experiences.

Other groups have visited the ruins of Machu Picchu in Peru, and ridden the Armu River, a fast-moving tributary in the heart of Siberia.

The company has also offered an Armu River trip in Primorye, Russia (for men and women), and a "Kidz to the River" trip for inner-city youth.

The common goal of Hawk's trips is the enrichment of the female spirit. "In a safe, supportive environment, without competition, women of all ages and degrees of experience are encouraged to recognize and appreciate their own physical and inner strengths and abilities," Beverly adds. "Our lives change, expand with the discovery that we are strong, durable, and capable of good judgment and effective action in a place where we once felt alien."

The spirituality of the great outdoors is also the focus of **Her Wild Song,** which offers wilderness trips for women only. Among their offerings are a winter stay at Little Lyford Pond Camps in Maine, where visitors can cross-country ski and go snowshoeing, as well as spring visits to the desert in Utah

(Escalante National Monument and Green River), where visitors can participate in Zen meditation sessions, canoeing, hiking, and backpacking (one of these excursions also allows men to come along).

As Joe put it, however, these types of excursions are not for everyone. They constitute a small segment of the travel market. But for the people who enjoy them, these trips can have a profound effect.

Resources

Carol Nashe Group, 617-437-9757, www.golfonthego.com
Hawk, I'm Your Sister, 505-984-2268, www.womansplace.com
Her Wild Song, 207-721-9005, www.herwildsong.org
Pete's Tours and Travel, 415-621-2915, http://home.pacbell.
net/psgreene
Rving Women, 888-55-RVING, www.rvingwomen.com
Spirit Journeys, 505-351-4004, www.spiritjourneys.com

Traveling With HIV and AIDS

People living with HIV deal with it in many different ways. Most people don't want to spend every vacation focusing on it. But for some, a vacation can provide the opportunity to learn new ways to deal with a difficult situation—and it can be a strengthening experience.

Many gay tour operators are well prepared to serve the needs of positive travelers, and while it is difficult to find a getaway specifically for HIV-positive people, travelers can try investigating group trips arranged by local AIDS and HIV organizations, or consider joining a meditation or spiritually focused group tour.

Check with your travel agent for other tours and packages.

As Bob, an HIV-positive man who's traveled the world, says, "I don't feel like I need to have workshops or anything like that, but I like the idea of going somewhere that help will be there if I need it."

TRAVEL TIP

Traveling With HIV

Concerns about health and travel are even more pronounced for people with HIV and AIDS, particularly when traveling abroad. Taking a few precautions, before and during your trip, will help make things go smoother.

• Before the trip, let your travel agent, travel planner, or tour operator know if you have specific needs or concerns.

• If traveling abroad, check with a consulate or embassy to see if there are any restrictions regarding entry for people with AIDS or HIV.

• Call the Centers for Disease Control at 404-639-3534 or visit www.cdc.gov for information about international travel.

• Check with your physician before any major trip to see if there are special precautions you should take related to your condition. He or she may suggest antidiarrheals, vaccines, or other medication to keep you as healthy as possible.

• If you're on medication, make sure you bring enough, plus a little bit extra, and be careful to adhere to the required schedule—just because you're on vacation doesn't mean you shouldn't take care of yourself. Bring a photocopy of your prescriptions in case of emergency.

• If you'll be flying through several time zones and are taking medication, check with your doctor about how to determine the schedule for when to take it.

• Consider the medical services available where you want to go. Is there sufficient support available if you need it? Travel agents and group tour organizers should be ready to answer any questions you may have. Also, consider medical evacuation insurance.

• As is good practice anywhere, avoid tap water, ice, and anything washed in water. Don't buy food products from street vendors.

• Don't swim in water that may be contaminated by sewage.

- Bring lots of sunblock or sunscreen. People with HIV are often more sensitive to damaging rays from the sun, so use lotion and cover yourself with shirts, hats, and sunglasses as much as possible.
- If insect bites are a risk at your destination, bring insect repellent and use it often.
- Find out if the region you're visiting has a local helpline or AIDS organization, in case you need help with an emergency referral.

The Wonderful World of Homosexuality— Gay Days at Amusement Parks

What started as an idea for a small group outing to Disney World has turned into an annual event that attracts thousands of gay men and lesbians from across the country and abroad.

"I don't think that first year I had any idea what it would turn into," says Doug Swallow, who founded the event in 1991. "We were on a computer bulletin board system in Orlando, and one of us had the idea that Disney would be a good place to go. The idea came to me to put up some flyers in Orlando."

Before he knew it, the event got written up in newspapers and mentioned on radio. "We got an awful lot of publicity," he recalls. The result? Instead of a couple dozen people that first year, Doug estimates there were 1,500 to 2,500.

For the second year, they decided to visibly identify themselves. "We came up with the slogan 'Wear red and be seen.'" Everyone was encouraged to meet around Cinderella's Castle at 3 P.M., after which they watched the parade going down Main Street.

So started a tradition that brings thousands of happy homos to the Disney theme parks in June, every year. The event now has its own official Web site—www.gaydays.com—that has complete information about the many events surrounding Gay Day, as well as links to more information and travel agents who can help book the trip. The Web site also has an extensive listing of other similar gay day-type events at other amusement parks throughout the country and abroad.

The number of attendees "more than triples every year," says Leila Hunter at Good Time Gay Productions, which offers packages. "It's a venue and a place where gay people can go for family fun—the gay and lesbian community is a family within itself. It's a place where everybody can be together and be themselves in a public venue that normally isn't considered a place where you see a bunch of gay people. The whole weekend isn't about politics or anything serious, it's just about a bunch of people having a good time and being together."

There are now other events scheduled to coincide with Gay Day at Disney. "We'll be running a bar bus at night," notes Leila. "Most all the events we're involved with are on Disney property or right near it." Doug adds that Universal Studios made an arrangement with Orlando's gay and lesbian community center to offer package deals that would include three nights' accommodation and admission to Universal Studios and Sea World.

Gay Day at Disney can be an ideal opportunity for gay parents to vacation with their kids. "We'll custom-make gay parents' packages," Leila says, noting that they devise alternate activities for gay parents and their kids while other people are barhopping.

Good Time, which has specialized in gay and lesbian travel exclusively since 1993, makes sure that the Orlando-area accommodations are gay-sensitive. "People have to understand this is a very different market," says Leila. "The packages that you give these people cannot just give lip service to the fact that they are gay and lesbian travelers. If we order a kingsize bed, we don't want our clients to be embarrassed when they check in."

Included in the package is admission to Gay Day at Disney, some meals and entertainment, plus a gay and lesbian "Fun Pack" with information about other attractions and activities of interest to lesbians and gays.

How does the Disney organization respond to this invasion of homosexuals? "It's pretty much an accepted thing now," says

Doug. "They publicly deny any active involvement, and they don't really have any. But individual managers have been very cooperative."

The problem with the growing popularity of the event, according to Doug, is that "we're in a little bit of a quandary. We're trying to find a way to spread ourselves out without *thinning* ourselves out." He recalls how at a recent gathering, "gays were the majority at the Magic Kingdom. They closed the gates."

Homosexual interest in Disney's creations is only natural, Doug theorizes. "We grew up with Disney—Mickey Mouse and Donald Duck and the feature movies with Cinderella and Snow White. And as you grow older, the opportunity to come back to a place that has childhood memories, and to do it with your friends and loved ones, has a major attraction as well."

The gay and lesbian community's enthusiasm for amusement parks has spread to many other locations around the world. If you can name an amusement park, there is probably some sort of a "gay day" when you can go with your favorite gay cohorts. Following is a partial listing of some of the events, with contact information:

Gay Day at Disneyland, Anaheim, Calif.; usually in October. www.gayday2.com

Gay & Lesbian Day at Waterworld, Concord, Calif.; usually in September. www.guspresents.com

Gay Day at Universal Studios Hollywood, Hollywood, Calif; usually in August. 888-UNIVERSAL, www.gaydayla.com

Colossus (Gay & Lesbian Night at Paramount's Great America), Santa Clara, Calif,; usually in May. www.guspresents.com

Gay Night at Six Flags Magic Mountain, Valencia, Calif.; www.odysseyadventures.com

Pearl Day at Six Flags Over Georgia, Atlanta, Ga.; usually in June. www.pearlday.com

Resources

Gaydays.com

Good Time Tours, 888-429-3527 or 305-864-9431, www.good timegaytravel.com

Odyssey Adventures, 818-893-2777, www.odysseyadven
tures.com

Tying the Knot—Gay Weddings Away From Home

When a judge in Hawaii ruled several years ago that it was unconstitutional for the state to deny gay people the right to marry, an awful lot of gay couples I know on the mainland were planning to hop over to Hawaii. And while gay and lesbian marriage is still not a reality in Hawaii, it has come closer in Vermont, which grants many of the same rights to same-sex couples as to gender-disconcordant heterosexual couplings (that's technical language that means straight couples).

As in several other gay-rights issues, the United States is behind some other countries in recognizing domestic partnerships. Gay couples were granted marriage rights in the Netherlands in 2001, and other countries that offer some (but not all) marriage rights include Canada, France, Germany, Norway, Sweden, and Denmark.

The extent to whch ceremonies held in other states or other countries will be recognized by officials back at home varies, but it's still not a bad idea to consider tying the knot. Even if insanely insecure legislators make it possible for other states to ignore our right to marry, the thought of one state—and a beautiful one at that—granting us the respect we've deserved all along is an exciting step in the right direction.

With all the recent controversy surrounding gay marriages, you'd think that the concept was something new. But lesbians and gay men have been formalizing their commitments for a long, long time, and there are more ways than ever to make the ceremony special, regardless of which states recognize it.

When Heide and Jen, both from California, decided it was time to tie the knot, they knew where they wanted to do it. "We had been to Hawaii on two previous occasions," Heide recalls, "and we thought if we were ever going to do a ceremony, then this would be the place to do it. It was going to be something private."

They had heard good things about the island of Maui, a lush tropical paradise that is known for its natural beauty more than its lesbian and gay community. The solitude, relaxed environment, sparkling clean beaches, and dramatic scenery made it seem like the perfect setting for saying their vows.

So they contacted **Royal Hawaiian Weddings** about two to three weeks before their arrival in Maui. "We told them we were looking for something simple, on a beach, at sunset. [Royal Hawaiian] got back to us and the ceremony was absolutely beautiful. It was on a small cove of beach that was completely deserted, on the southeast end of the island."

The two women didn't need active nightlife or a large lesbian community. "We weren't looking for anything like that," explains Heide. They had chosen Maui because, "It's very easy-going, it's not like you have to run around and make sure you hit all the landmarks. The people are very welcoming. And there's a sense of calm, even in Lahaina—it's a small town and it's not resortish."

Royal Hawaiian arranged the ceremony, but not the rest of the trip. "They gave us instructions on how to get to the location of the ceremony. We didn't really want anything, really, just a small ceremony. But there are a lot of other options. You can have champagne and cake, and my understanding is that they do ceremonies for straight people as well."

Indeed, Royal Hawaiian offers six choices to make the ceremony as simple or as grandiose as you want it. The "Just Maui Me" package includes the use of a secluded beach location, a state-licensed minister or officiant, and a copy of the wedding vows and/or wedding certificate.

A mid-priced "Private Elegance" package also includes thirty-six four-by-six-inch photos in an album, a musician, two deluxe floral leis, champagne or cider, two champagne flutes, and an on-site coordinator. The top of the line is the "Romance Over Dinner" package, which includes a wedding cake, an edited wedding video, and a private four-course sunset candlelight dinner for two on a secluded beach after the ceremony.

Heide points out that Royal Hawaiian works with couples to create the kind of ceremony they want—large or small, religious or secular. Before they even left the mainland, Heide and Jen were able to approve by fax the vows they would recite.

She thinks that increased controversy over gay marriage may increase the amount of marriage traffic into Hawaii, although it didn't influence her and Jen. "That's not why we did it. We did it because it was a beautiful place and because it was time to get married. What better place to commit than on a beach, with the sunset, and the peace and tranquility?"

For gay and lesbian fiancés unable to make the trek all the way to Hawaii, there are a growing number of options throughout North America. Major gay tour operators haven't come up with many wedding options yet, but an increasing number of smaller inns and bed and breakfast properties have devised their own programs.

The Internet can be a great resource in finding out about some of the latest legal and travel details. Gayweddings.com, for example, includes information about gay wedding packages in Vermont and in other locations, as well as assistance with planning, listings of wedding planners and legal information. The site is also home to the Gay Wedding Store, which sells items like glassware, albums, guest books and other goodies. Rainbowunions.com is another similar site, with basic information about planning a wedding; it also has a vendor directory of gay-friendly commitment ceremony specialists.

For destination-specific information about the legal status of gay marriage, you can visit sites like www.hawaiilawyer.com, which provides updates about the struggle in Hawaii. Gaywed dingguide.com is a Vermont-based Web site that provides a forum for businesses catering to people interested in gay and lesbian wedding ceremonies, including listings of accommodations, catering, photographers, clergy, florists and other businesses. The site also has a wedding gift registry and details about Vermont's gay marriage laws.

Many individual hotels offer gay and lesbian wedding packages. The North Hero House, for example, offers a variety of options for couples, allowing you to choose anything from an intimate ceremony to a celebration for up to 180 people. The North Hero House has a justice of the peace on staff who is licensed to conduct a civil ceremony on site. Other Vermont properties with packages include the Summit Lodge, in Killington, and Sugar Lodge at Sugarbush, in Warren.

For other ideas, ask your travel agent or call smaller, gay-friendly establishments near your destination.

Resources

Aloha Lambda Weddings, 800-982-5176, www.global-aloha.com/gayweddings

Gay Wedding Guide, www.gayweddingguide.com

Gay Weddings, www.gayweddings.com

Hawaii Lawyer, www.hawaiilawyer.com

North Hero House, 888-565-3644, www.northherohouse.com

Rainbow Unions, http://rainbowunions.com

Royal Hawaiian Weddings, 800-659-1866, www.royalhawaiianweddings.com

Sugar Lodge at Sugarbush, 800-982-3465, www.vermontgayandlesbianweddings.com

Summit Lodge, 800-635-6343, www.summitlodgevermont.com

Dungeons and Antiques—The Diverse World of Travel Keys Tours

When Peter Manston isn't leading groups of leathermen through the torture chambers of Europe, you may very well find him leading a more sedate group of travelers through some of the most popular flea markets in London.

That's part of his job as head of **Travel Keys Tours,** a company that offers both dungeon tours for leathermen and antiquing tours for flea market aficionados.

They're both natural markets, Peter says.

When you consider the elaborate scenarios played out by some leather enthusiasts, it seems only natural that they might feel at home in the dungeons of Europe, where similar, albeit more serious, variations on their activities took place long ago.

This is the reasoning behind "Dungeons and Castles of Europe: The Leatherman's Tour," a package offered once a year by Sacramento-based Travel Keys Tours.

The annual excursion grew out of group leader Peter Manston's own personal passion. "It's something I've been interested in as long as I can remember," he explains. "I'd tell people about things that I'd done at assorted castles and dungeons, and they would say, 'Gosh, can you take me?' " Finally, in 1990, he put together his first packaged tour.

The thirteen-day trip is limited to twenty men and begins in Frankfurt, roaming throughout the region with stops in Amsterdam for visits to several leather clubs; Ghent, Belgium, for a visit to Gravesteen Castle, "one of the finest torture museums" in Europe; The Hague, for a tour of a sixteenth-century prison; Nürnberg, for a look at an underground torture chamber and dungeon; plus two nights in Berlin for a tour of the city's vibrant "leather life." Nighttime activities include several visits to bars and pubs with equipment-filled backrooms and cellars.

The accommodations for most of the trip stay within the theme. "We stay at castles, one along the river. You go right over the moat and through the drawbridge."

The trip is always timed to arrive in Munich in time for the Oktoberfest, which runs simultaneously with a leather festival. "There is an emphasis on beer drinking, dancing, and eating," says Peter, noting that even those who don't drink can enjoy the festivities with a good-tasting nonalcoholic brew. "The leather contingent has a balcony reserved in the beer hall overlooking the festivities. I can't think of anything that exactly compares to it."

The tour price includes all lodging, ground transportation, admission to castles, dungeons and museums, as well as all breakfasts and some lunches and dinners.

The tour is marketed as a leatherman's tour, but Peter says the types of people vary. "Some people wear leather the whole time," he says, "but it's not required."

Peter says that women are not invited on the tours primarily because "This is not just a museum tour; we go out, and a lot of the places we go to won't let women in."

Peter speaks German, French, and Italian, and is ready to help with translations. He's even available to help introduce people to the "scenes" that interest them. But everyone has a different idea about what they want from a trip like this, he explains, and from time to time he finds a traveler disappointed because they had expected to be involved in heavy S&M scenes every night of the trip. "I can take you to the places where that might happen," Peter says, "and I can introduce you to people, but I can't do everything."

Leather enthusiast or not, the traveler is sure to come away with a sense of history. "Only in the late eighteenth century, about the time of the Marquis de Sade, did dungeons become places of play," Peter writes in his brochure. "After seeing the 'for-real' devices and places on this tour, you may have new ideas to reproduce or adapt for your own use."

Equally intense as far as antiquers are concerned, is Travel Keys' other tour, called "Flea Markets, Antiques Fairs, and Auctions of Europe." The tour takes people—both gay and straight—to England and France for some intense shopping. The package is aimed at people interested not in general city tours, but in searching out crafts, antiques, and artwork.

The tour begins in London, with visits to the New Caledonian/Bermondsey Street market, the Portobello Road tourists' market, the Camden Lock market, and the Jubilee Market, one of London's few indoor antiques markets. Next, the group heads north to Yorkshire, Lancashire, and Birmingham to visit antiques warehouses. In Paris, attractions include the Louvre des Antiquitaires, "a museum where everything's for sale"; the Hotel Drouot, a bustling auction house; the Porte de Vanves, a mid-range flea market; and the Clignancourt Marché aux Puces, "the greatest single flea market in the world. Thousands of vendors offer every type of merchandise you can imagine."

The travelers on this trip may be a bit different from Travel Keys' dungeon tours, but gay and lesbian travelers are sure to

---

TRAVEL TIP

Traveling Healthy

My friend Ivan was worried about getting *turista*—you know, Montezuma's revenge, that infamous traveler's diarrhea—during an upcoming trip to Mexico. "I was so worked up about it," he says, "that I got the runs three days before I even started the trip!"

Such is the influence that the mind wields over the body. So the first thing you should pack for a healthy trip is a healthy mindset.

Vacation travel can produce a great deal of stress. Combine time differences, stale airplane cabin air, unusual scheduling, and the fact that people are often tired and stressed out before they even *begin* their trips, and you've got a recipe for trouble. Remember, the point of vacation travel is supposed to be relaxation and enjoyment. Take time to slow down from your normal pace at some point before, during, and after your vacation.

Step two is taking care of your body. You'll need to be particularly careful in foreign countries. Here are a few general tips:

• Eat protein for energy, especially in the mornings and afternoons.

• Avoid unhealthy treats—don't completely give up your healthy diet.

• Don't give up your exercise routine, either. If you usually work out in a gym, you should still do push-ups and sit-ups, and take walks to keep your body going.

• In developing countries, water should be treated either by boiling it or by using tablets to kill bacteria before drinking. Bottled water is usually safest. Don't forget to order your drinks without ice. Salads, uncooked vegetables, and unpeeled fruits are also on the no-no list if you want to avoid *turista.*

• Check ahead of time to see if any vaccines are required for your destination. Hepatitis shots before leaving are probably a good idea no matter where you're going.

• Bring insect repellent to protect yourself from potentially dangerous insect bites.

- Take a look at your medical coverage. Does it cover you abroad? If not, consider purchasing a travel insurance policy.
- Remember to bring along the necessary equipment (condoms, dental dams, etc.) if you think you may be sexually active during your vacation. Attitudes toward sex vary in different parts of the world, and even from resort to resort. It's up to you to protect yourself and to be responsible to those with whom you come into contact.

---

feel at home. With antiquing, "there are always gay people on the trip," Peter says.

Resources

Travel Keys Tours, 916-452-5200

Traveling With the Kids

Gays and lesbians with kids who want to take a group tour usually end up doing it with a "mainstream" group. But there are a few options for gay parents who would like to be in a "pro-gay" environment that is also fun for kids. The "gay day" events held at many major amusement parks across the country (see the separate section about this) can be a good opportunity for both you and your little ones to enjoy the delights of Snow White.

In addition, other tour operators offer "kid-friendly" tours from time to time. **Adventures in Good Company** has offered a "Take Your Daughter to Play Week" package, for women and girls only. The trip is designed for mothers who want to spend more time with their daughters "in a setting where they don't have to be in charge or do the cooking." Activities include paddling down lazy rivers and camping; daughters should be between 13 and 17 years of age.

Resources

Adventures in Good Company, 651-998-0120 or 877-439-4042, www.goodadventure.com

5

THE RESORT EXPERIENCE

"Follow the yellow brick road."

—The Munchkins in "The Wizard of Oz"

I've visited several mainstream resorts in Jamaica that claim to fulfill the needs of every vacationer: they've got Caribbean breezes to caress your face, powdery white beaches to cushion your behind, and fruity drinks served by an attentive staff.

But they lack one thing: happy homosexuals.

Anyone who wonders why gay and lesbian resorts are necessary has never tried to kiss someone of the same sex on a public beach, or to meet a gay person in a hotel's straight disco. There are some gorgeous mainstream resorts out there—places that offer great weather, beautiful surroundings, plenty of activities, and outstanding accommodations—but it's just no fun to spend money and free time in a resort where you're not going to feel comfortable, or where your kind isn't even wanted.

Until fairly recently, we were left with not much choice besides the major gay and lesbian vacation destinations like Provincetown and Palm Springs. Homosexuals have traditionally gravitated toward the more accepting urban areas where space didn't allow such development. But now, gays and lesbians can select a resort experience of the same quality as their straight counterparts, in a wide variety of settings.

That's right, you can find your gay brothers and sisters *en masse* in a variety of resorts, lodges, and camps—some are places where you wouldn't ordinarily expect to see many gay people.

The facilities vary quite a bit, but their commonalities reflect the basic needs of gay travelers (which, lo and behold, are quite similar to those of straight people). The definition of the word "resort" is open to discussion. Some properties slap the word onto their name so they'll seem bigger or more luxurious than they really are. For the purpose of this book, we'll define a resort as a hotel facility that is reasonably self-contained, meaning that you could feasibly stay on the property all day. Several amenities and activities should be available on-site, including a pool, hot tub, Jacuzzi, sauna, and perhaps some outdoor sports. Resorts are usually far from major urban areas. Within the listings, I've also included several clothing-optional accommodations, which may not offer as many extras as true resorts, but which nevertheless serve a resortlike function for the people who stay there. This, I realize, is a fairly liberal definition of the word "resort," but better to include too much than too little, right?

The largest facilities are generally the mainstream resorts "chartered out" by gay tour operators. **Atlantis** is one of the oldest companies offering all-gay, "all-inclusive" resort vacations. Their Atlantis at **Club Med** packages turn the facilities of the well-known resort chain into an all-gay paradise. The inclusive package includes meals, sports, activities, entertainment, and parties, all for one weekly rate. **Olivia** does the same thing for women at several resorts.

Other than Club Med, most mainstream resorts don't have "all-gay" packages available, although this is likely to change as resorts scramble to fill their rooms.

Many people aren't even looking for a big Caribbean-style resort—a small place tucked out of the way right here in the

United States is fine. The Timberfell Lodge, for example, offers 250 secluded acres in eastern Tennessee for gay men, with heaping helpings of natural beauty to soothe the nerves of the most frazzled urbanite (and lest one become *too* relaxed, they've got leather-inspired activities to shake things up). Another property with unique activities is Hateful Missy and Granny Butch's Boudoir and Manure Emporium (yes, that's the actual name!). Located about thirty-five minutes from Albuquerque, New Mexico, this two-story adobe bed and breakfast suggests pastimes that include commitment ceremonies, amiable divorces, shooting pool, shoveling manure, and slapping hogs. Hey, it takes all kinds.

Because of the great variety of resort vacations now offered, you'll find the resource listings divided. Some of the smaller properties may not consist of much more than some guest rooms and a hot tub—but for many people, that's enough!

THINGS TO THINK ABOUT FIRST   What kind of environment are you looking for—relaxed, fast-paced, men/women, ultraluxurious, sexually frisky, clothing optional? Do you want a location with lots of activities available off the property, or are you looking for a self-sufficient, isolated getaway? What kind of weather and outdoor activities do you prefer?

QUESTIONS TO ASK THE TRAVEL PROVIDER   Is the property exclusively male/female, gay/straight? What is included in the overall price—airfare, activities, meals, drinks, ground transfers for guests arriving by plane? What are your cancellation/refund policies? What kinds of activities/facilities are available on the property? Which of the resort's facilities are on the property and which are in each room? Are excursions available outside the property? Where is the property located in relation to other sites of interest? Are visitors mostly couples/singles/men/women? Will straight people be staying there, too?

The All-Inclusive Vacation— Atlantis and Club RSVP

Several times a year, the lush enclaves of a few **Club Med** resorts take on a certain gay sensibility.

The straight discos sway to the beat of tea dances, the entertainers start singing homosexual favorites (gasp!), and the men have better haircuts than the average Club Med guest.

It's **Atlantis** at Club Med, a vacation made for gay aficionados of the all-inclusive concept.

"You get to meet so many people," says Rich Volo, fresh from a visit to Atlantis at Club Med Cancun. Rich is a firm believer in the value of all-inclusive vacations, and an even firmer believer that the only way to do it is with a bunch of homos.

"The only way I'd ever visit an all-inclusive resort is with an all-gay group," Rich continues. "With a gay group, you can do things that really interest you. What other resorts have a tea dance? Where else can you see Michael Feinstein?" Indeed, name-brand entertainment and attention to the needs of gay and lesbian travelers help make all-inclusive resorts an increasingly popular choice.

With an all-inclusive vacation, you can leave your wallet in your room and enjoy the beach, the waterskiing, the disco—whatever strikes your fancy. Many people favor the all-inclusive concept because it helps keep the vacation within a predetermined budget.

And our all-inclusive options have gotten brighter since the beginning of the 1990s. Their packages include accommodations, three meals a day, unlimited beer and wine with lunch and dinner, sports, organized activities, entertainment, nightclub activities, special events and tips, gratuities, and taxes. Some packages include alcoholic beverages all day and night.

A variety of rates are available depending on location—the Club Atlantis at Blue Bay Village, located on Mexico's Pacific Coast, is the least expensive property to visit, but still offers a mile-long private beach, a full schedule of entertainment and activities, plus cultural and shopping excursions. The three-story hotel features rooms with balconies, televisions, phones, and private bathrooms. Deluxe apartments, bungalows, and suites are available at a higher price.

Amenities and activities at the fifty-square-mile property include two swimming pools, tennis (on three courts), sailing, horseback riding on the beach, scuba lessons, windsurfing, kayaking, snorkeling, volleyball, and aerobics. For an extra fee, guests can participate in deep-sea fishing, sunset cruises, and waterskiing. Two restaurants offer a variety of cuisine, while a nightclub keeps night owls up 'til the wee hours.

Atlantis has also offered packages at Club Med Eleuthera. Located in the Bahamas, the resort offers a host of activities, including a circus workshop, allowing you to fulfill your dreams of becoming a trapeze artist. Accommodations are air-conditioned and located in two-story structures with either garden or beach views. Some have connecting rooms and king-sized beds.

On the property, guests have easy access to beaches and a Caribbean marina and water sports center that offers waterskiing, windsurfing and snorkeling. Other activities include tennis, practice golf, volleyball, aerobics, and softball. Additional features include an open-air cocktail lounge, outdoor dance floor, nightclub, and theater. For an additional fee, scuba diving is available off the property, as are cultural excursions to Nassau and Harbour Island.

The priciest package has been Atlantis's Daydream Island, off the coast of Australia. This package incorporated a five-day visit to Sydney's famed Gay and Lesbian Mardi Gras, followed by a visit to this private island on the Great Barrier Reef. "It's the perfect way to see both the cities and the natural beauty of this fantastic continent," the people at Atlantis promise.

In Sydney, guests stay at either the four-star Hyde Park Plaza or the five-star Marriott and partake in Sydney's largest gay celebration, followed by a bunch of so-called recovery parties. Then it's time to hop on a short flight, followed by a short boat ride, to Daydream, Atlantis's forty-one-acre private island. The resort, located on the island's northern tip, features in-room television, radio, phone, minibar, refrigerator, in-room movies, and a private bathroom. Three beaches and two swimming pools beckon, as well as windsurfing, catamarans, snorkeling, water polo, aqua aerobics, and fishing. Parasailing, waterskiing, and scuba diving on the Great Barrier Reef can be arranged for an extra charge. The property also features saunas and spas, three restaurants, and a nightclub.

A typical day at an Atlantis resort might include scuba diving, tennis, waterskiing, or just sunbathing on the beach. Nighttime generally heats up with name-brand entertainment and theme parties, and well-known DJs from throughout the United States. The crowd tends to be a mixed age group of singles and couples, the overall mood relaxed yet festive. You won't have any problem finding parties every night.

Like any vacation, large all-inclusive resorts aren't for everyone. They're not recommended for adventure-seeking people interested in exploring nature or new cultures, because most of the vacation is spent in a protected compound that has little to do with life outside. Also, these resorts tend to be filled with fellow visitors from the United States, so you have to find your own way to meet the locals.

"I wouldn't want to take every vacation at an all-inclusive," notes Enrico. "It's a little mindless sometimes. But for sheer relaxation and the opportunity to do water sports and party in a really nice, tropical setting, you can't beat it."

Resources

Atlantis Events, 800-6-ATLANTIS, www.atlantisevents.com
RSVP, 800-328-RSVP, www.rsvp.net

The All-Inclusive Vacation—Olivia at Club Med

Fredda Rubin admits that she and her lover, Katia Soares Netto, made a mistake the first time they planned an all-inclusive vacation: They stayed at a straight resort.

"It was very pretty, very nice, but we felt like fish out of water," she says about their trip to Ciboney, an all-inclusive mainstream resort in Ocho Rios, Jamaica. "We just stood around on the outskirts and watched these [straight] people. I had to respect the fact that my lover didn't want to dance with me on New Year's Eve."

They never made that mistake again. Fredda and Katia spent their next resort vacation at Club Med in Playa Blanca, Mexico, on an all-woman getaway with **Olivia Cruises and Resorts.** "It was even better than I had expected," she recalls. "They charter out a whole Club Med. The food was great; there's beautiful beaches so there's snorkeling, scuba diving. Plus, there's horseback riding, tennis. They even put on a circus, which included guests. I was in the arts and crafts program and I made a silk scarf."

Best of all, of course, Fredda and Katia didn't have to worry about fitting in. "They played the Newlywed Game and the Dating Game, with women," she says, noting that there were plenty of single women and couples to play both games.

Other activities included pool games, volleyball, and basketball. Since their vacation took place during the popular Cinco de Mayo festival, local bands and dancers also came to the property to perform.

The two women had such a good time, in fact, that they returned again. The trip they're currently planning, meanwhile, is another Olivia-run trip, this time to Club Med in Sonora Bay, Mexico. Olivia regularly introduces new packages with various Club Med locations.

The Olivia holidays at Club Med are nearly identical in concept to those offered by Atlantis—you pay one price for just about everything, then relax and enjoy yourself.

So what would Fredda say to a gay person who decided to go on a straight tour to save some money? "I would say, 'Every day, you live in a straight world. If you really enjoy doing that on a vacation, good luck to you. Part of my pleasure derives from being with my people.'"

Resources

Olivia Cruises and Resorts, 800-631-6277, www.Olivia.com

South Pacific Paradise—Man Friday Resort

Think, for a moment, of that vast paradise known as the South Pacific. What visions come to mind? If you're thinking about that song, "I'm Going to Wash That Man Right Out of My Hair," you're dating yourself. If you know about Man Friday Resort, you're right on track.

Man Friday is Fiji's first all-gay resort, offering ten acres of manicured gardens and rain forest on a private peninsula extending from Fiji's Coral Coast. "It's so beautiful, it's just awesome," says Don Edwards, who's visited the property once (booking through **Men on Vacation**) and would love to do it again. "The beach is great, and the resort is all grass and vegetation."

Fiji, which is located a few hours beyond Hawaii, is a small island graced with beaches, sunshine, rain forests, and coral reefs. It can be reached via nonstop service from Los Angeles and San Francisco, as well as Hawaii. While the trip may be several hours, it doesn't take guests long to fall into the casual, relaxed atmosphere of Man Friday. Before they know it, they're tying a *sulu*—the traditional Fijian wraparound garment—around their bathing suit and joining right in.

Guests—both gay men and lesbians—are encouraged to set their own pace at Man Friday. "They have planned activities every day," Don notes. "But you can pick and choose as you like." Guests enjoy swimming in the freshwater pool or the sparkling waters of the Pacific Ocean. Free waterskiing is available for one hour per day, depending on the tides. Snorkeling, windsurfing, glass-bottom boating, and fishing are all available at the resort. And a permanent divemaster is on the property.

If you've had enough of the water, you can play tennis or volleyball, go horseback riding or jogging, or lie out in the sun. Nature hikes to nearby waterfalls are also popular ways to unwind.

Entertainment includes a variety of games, competitions, and musical performances nightly. Every week, guests are treated to a *Meke,* a performance of traditional Fijian dance and song, and a *Lovo,* the traditional Fijian variation on a barbecue.

Don notes that a vacation at Man Friday can be filled with activities or lazing in the sun. Just don't expect heavy-duty partying. In fact, Fiji offers no gay nightife outside of the resort. "It's not an overly decadent atmosphere," he explains. "It's not wandering around in the bushes or that sort of thing. I would think this would be for a more mature, hardworking sophisticated crowd [he estimates such a crowd would be in their mid-thirties and up] that wants rest with a little activity—and who is also inquisitive about the life on the island."

Indeed, the resort boasts about its integration with local villagers, who are a multicultural mix of Fijian, Indian, Chinese, and European descent. They staff the resort, and guests also have the chance to learn more about life on the island with day trips to local settlements. "You get to interact with the natives in the village," says Don, who enjoyed speaking with women in the village and learning about their customs and traditions, which include pottery making. You may also find yourself learning more about Australia and New Zealand, because Fiji is a popular destination for travelers both gay and straight from these nations, as well.

Air-conditioned coaches are available to provide tours of Sigatoka Valley, Pacific Harbour, and Orchid Island, along with the chance to catch up on some duty-free shopping. But even with the shopping opportunities, Don says, "it's not an overly commercial atmosphere. You just go there to enjoy being quiet."

Guests stay in individual units, called *bures,* which are "really quite nice inside," Edwards reports. "The bedrooms had been completely remodeled."

Meals are taken at Crusoe's, the property's on-site restaurant. A daily tropical breakfast is included in the package prices, and meals include fresh local seafood, fruits, and juices.

To help even out the mix of Man Friday guests, the majority of whom are men, women's weeks and family weeks are also offered. The goal is to keep everyone happy.

Don says they've already achieved that goal. "There's no way you could be dissatisfied with it," he says, "unless you're expecting party time."

For travelers who *are* looking for some party time to mix in with their relaxation, Man Friday can serve as a logical and refreshing stopover en route to or from the Sydney Gay and Lesbian Mardi Gras. Men on Vacation and **Above and Beyond Tours** have both offered an add-on to Mardi Gras package tours that includes a visit to Fiji. They can also plan personalized itineraries for more independent travelers.

Resources

Above and Beyond, 800-397-2681 or 415-284-1666, www.above beyondtours.com
Men on Vacation, 800-959-4636, www.menonvacation.com

Paradise Off the Beaten Track

When it comes time to plan a gay vacation, the biggest gay destinations—places like South Beach and Provincetown—get most of the attention, because of their wide variety of accommodations, bars, clubs, and beaches.

But our community isn't limited to the largest cities and most densely gay resort towns. We can have our fun just about anywhere, given an attractive setting and sympathetic hosts. And there are a whole bunch of gay and lesbian resorts in places you might not expect to find them. Many people who've discovered these out-of-the-way places find them an ideal alternative to the larger gay and lesbian hotspots.

These hideaways are tucked away in places like Tennessee, Ohio, and Arizona, where you might not expect to find a gay haven. But that's what helps to make them stand out: an unlikely location, a laid-back atmosphere, a lack of outside distractions—and, often, a clothing-optional policy.

"It's very hard to compare this to Palm Springs or anything else," says John Searle, a guest at **Timberfell Lodge,** a men-only resort in the Smokey Mountains of eastern Tennessee. John likes the experience so much that he's visited twice, traveling all the way from his home in Australia.

"It's completely different and very isolated, up in the mountains," he explains. "I've never stayed at anything quite like this. There's not anything nearby, so you stay on the property. You can go for a bushwalk, swimming, sauna, Jacuzzi. There's plenty of things to do. The main idea is to come here and relax."

"I like the opportunity to get away and relax," agrees Lee from Texas, who was visiting Timberfell for the fourth time. "I'm not really a bar person. I like the quietness, the serenity, the nature. At night you can hear the frogs and the crickets. Being from the city, it's a nice change."

These guys can thank the failed relationship of Timberfell's owner, David Yoder, for spurring the development of the lodge. Several years ago, David and his lover, both Californians, had been drawn to Tennessee by its low property prices. They ended up buying 250 acres of tree-covered mountain hollow.

"Then, when we broke up," David explains, "I decided to rent out rooms in our four-bedroom house to make money." Since then, the resort has grown to twenty-nine beds. There are private bedrooms in the lodge and six rooms in the annex building, ranging from shared bunk rooms for three or four people to the deluxe room, with queen-sized bed, sitting area, television, phone, private bath, and a refrigerator.

Breakfast and dinner are included in the nightly price; lunch is available for an additional charge. "The food is always very good," says Lee. "You get a full dinner, with wine and dessert."

Sites are also available for campers with tents and recreational vehicles, although campers must pay extra for lodge privileges.

During the day, guests usually spend a decent amount of time at the pool, and may hike some of the nature trails that crisscross the property. Visitors with cars often make the ninety-mile trip to visit the Biltmore estate in Asheville, North Carolina (one of the most impressive private residences in the nation), or to Dollywood in Pigeon Forge, Tennessee (an ode to that bewigged country music star, Dolly Parton). During the summer months, whitewater rafting is nearby, and in the winter, skiing is the preferred off-property activity.

Even without the activities, Lee says that the social environment is a big draw. "On a busy weekend, there will be probably one hundred people or more. You meet people, make friends. Some of the same people return here each year."

"Also," he adds, "it's nudist if you want." Indeed, the entire resort is clothing-optional, although Lee says that most of the naked people can be found near the pool, Jacuzzi, and sauna. "Most people dress for dinner," he reports.

Owner David Yoder says that the diverse male clientele includes a mix of singles and couples from all over the country, about 15 percent of which is "into the leather scene."

"Timberfell is different because it's a *destination,* rather than people just stopping off," notes Yoder. That's a common thread between most of the gay and lesbian resorts that we find off the beaten path: People plan their vacations around the resort itself and spend most of their time on the property, rather than using it as simply a resting place or a base for other activities. Because of the greater isolation, these resorts tend to be more self-sufficient.

If you're looking for something a bit off the beaten track, check the list at the end of this chapter.

Accommodations

Timberfell Lodge   2240 Van Hill Rd., Greenville, TN 37745; 800-437-0118 or 423-234-0844, www.timberfell.com (men only, 29 rooms, $94 and up, camping, $35). Accommodations here vary by price and amenities, ranging from rooms with private baths, refrigerators, and TV, to a twelve-person bunk room filled with double beds.

At One With Nature, the Hawaiian Way

Even before the state began discussing gay marriage, gays and lesbians had a long-running love affair with Hawaii. Now, the 113-acre **Kalani Oceanside Eco-Resort** offers us the chance to learn more about the islands, while learning more about what goes on inside the body and mind.

Kalani, located on the southeast shore of the Big Island, is the only coastal lodging facility within Hawaii's largest conservation area. The facility is actually a nonprofit, educational organization. Amid the lush tropical beauty of Hawaii, you can partake in a number of programs, some offered by other organizations. For example:

The *"Body Electric" package* promises to "explore deeper feelings and erotic energy within, and with a community of fellow seekers," through conscious breathwork and sacred rituals. Also available is a "Body Erotic" program, which provides a "soulful, sensual totally male massage" for men only.

You can even deepen your spiritual understanding while shaking your booty. The *"Gay Spirit Gathering"* is "a fabulous tribal celebration and transformative alternative to the *holidaze*. Hips will roll to rhythms of hula, as your spirit reflects the serenity of the islands."

The *"Men's Adventure Camp" program* features hikes to secluded beaches, and the opportunity to go spelunking in lava caves, kayak through streams into the sea, swim under waterfalls, feel hot lava, plunge in crater lakes and thermal springs, etc. It will, the resort says, awaken "soulful, sensual, deep brotherhood."

The *"Hula Festival,"* meanwhile, lets guests explore traditional dance, chants, myths, crafts, and language, by attending a cultural exposition called the Merrie Monarch Hula Festival.

"I-MEN," which stands for International Men Enjoying Naturism, has also offered a program of activities for nudists.

Programs especially for women (but not just lesbians) include "Goddess Myths of Hawaii," an exploration of art, music, dance, yoga, massage, and story.

"Women's Earth/Spirit Renewal" features water massage and release rituals. Another program focuses on eating disorders and compulsions as well as body image problems.

Guests can choose from accommodations in cottages, lodges, or campsites. The resort specializes in healthful cuisine, therapeutic massage, "stimulating seminars," and other activities. On the property is a spa featuring a sauna, Jacuzzi, massages, and a twenty-five-meter Olympic-sized pool, plus a reading room and weights. Films, games, snorkel, and sports equipment are also available.

A host of other activities and programs are open to all, including yoga, Tai Chi, and swimming with the dolphins that frequent a nearby beach. The sea cliffs of the Kalani coast area provide vantage points for viewing the whales that spend their winters nearby. Other attractions nearby include the Volcanoes National Park, thermal springs, steam vents, snorkeling tidal pools, a crater lake, and five parks.

Accommodations

Kalani Oceanside Eco-Resort RR2, Box 4500, Kehena Beach, HI 96778; 800-800-6886. www.kalani.com (mixed gay/straight resort with specific programs that are men-only and women-only; also vacation rentals, artist residencies, and volunteer programs). Ocean vista cottages, lodges, campsites, Olympic-sized pool, spa, naturist beaches, thermal springs, snorkeling, kayaking; close to waterfalls, volcanoes, and other natural attractions.

Camping It Up

No, not that kind of camp. The outdoor kind.

Remember how much fun camping used to be when you were little? Okay, okay, for a lot of us, it wasn't fun (people always made fun of me because I couldn't tie a square knot). But now's your chance to revisit that experience and finally discover the fun you had missed.

"I like the chance to get away from everything, just to escape with some friends and pitch a tent somewhere," says Kent, who relishes his once-a-year trips away from the urban excitement of Kansas City. "We hike, we play volleyball and swim, we just hang out. And, it's a lot cheaper than other kinds of vacations at expensive resorts."

Maybe one of the reasons that activities like camping haven't caught on quicker with our community is that we frequently feel unwelcome, sometimes even in danger, outside our standard gay enclaves. Thanks to the conservative views that sometimes permeate the less populated areas where people camp, safety is as much a concern for lesbians and gay men in the country as in the city; frequenting rustic settings can be even more dangerous than walking down a dark alley in the biggest city.

These worries are minimized in a gay-friendly campground. When you know ahead of time the place you're staying will welcome you, you're more likely to feel comfortable and relaxed once you get there.

Gay and gay-friendly campgrounds dot this great nation of ours, so next time you pack up the car for a road trip, consider skipping the Red Roof Inn for something a little closer to nature. Tents and other essential materials can easily be rented from camping supply stores; those with dreams of Winnebagos can even rent a large-scale recreational RV that is totally self-sufficient.

Don't think you'll necessarily have to leave all the big-city fun behind when you head into the country. **Oneida Campground & Lodge,** in New Milford, Pennsylvania, stages drag shows during the weekends, and the property's own dance hall, the Club House, also allows for nighttime fun. Established in 1980, Oneida claims to be the oldest and only gay-owned and operated campground. The property is located on one hundred acres in the mountains of northeastern Pennsylvania and offers numerous campsites in the woods, most of which have water and electricity. Rooms are available for rent at one of two lodges, and rental cabins and trailers are also available. Guests keep clean at three bathhouses with modern facilities, as well as a sauna. Activities include volleyball and swimming at a private dock along the shore of East Lake. In addition to the drag shows and dancing, evening activities include gathering around a big, old-fashioned bonfire.

Oneida also offers a series of gay-specific events throughout its open season, from March to October. Among the interesting offerings: Prom Weekend in June, when you can relive the prom experience with your lover; Nudity Weekend, also in June, which is pretty self-explanatory; and the Miss Oneida Pageant in August. Leather/Levi and gay pride events take place at various times, as well.

Camping has entered the organized gay tour industry, as well. Several tour operators offer escorted camping trips to various regions of the world, particularly to the western United States.

Escorted tours are especially nice for inexperienced campers who aren't sure what to expect. With many such tours, you don't even have to have any equipment; you can rent all the necessary items for an outdoor adventure.

OutWest Adventures, for example, offers group tours that feature camping in the mountains of Montana and Utah. **Toto Tours** and **Spirit Journeys** offer men-only trips that feature camping. Companies that offer the same for women only include **Mariah Wilderness Expeditions, Hawk, I'm Your Sister, Her Wild Song,** and **Woodswomen.**

Most camping tours involve other outdoor activities as well, such as whitewater rafting and hiking; see the section called "Riding the Rapids" in the Active Vacations chapter and the chapter on Special Interest Tours for details.

THINGS TO THINK ABOUT FIRST   Do you like the outdoors? What kind of outdoor activities do you like? Is there a gay-friendly campground near the route you're taking? How much do you want to rough it (can you do without electricity, or do you need a campground with lots of outlets for your hair dryer)?

QUESTIONS TO ASK THE TRAVEL PROVIDER   Is the clientele exclusively gay/lesbian? Are reservations refundable? Do you have the facilities for tents/campers/electricity? What sort of bathroom/shower facilities are provided? Do you charge per person or by vehicle? Are there any activities available at the site or nearby? What sort of security is there at the facility? (For tours: What activities and meals are included?)

Resources

Hawk, I'm Your Sister, 505-984-2268, www.womansplace.com
Her Wild Song, 207-586-5986
Mariah Wilderness Expeditions, 800-462-7424 or 510-233-2303, www.mariahwe.com
OutWest Adventures, 800-743-0458, www.outwestadventure.com
Spirit Journeys, 505-351-4004
Toto Tours, 800-565-1241 or 773-274-8686, 8695 fax www.tototours.com

Unexpected Pleasures

The following is a sampling of gay and lesbian "resorts," guest houses, and campgrounds outside the standard gay tourist areas:

Arizona Sunburst Inn   6245 North 12th Pl., Phoenix, AZ 85014; 800-974-1474 or 602-274-1474; www.azsunburst (men only, 7 units, clothing optional, $69 and up). This bed and breakfast features a pool and a hot tub.

Aurora Winds Resort B&B   7501 Upper O'Malley, Anchorage, AK 99516; 907-346-2533 fax 907-346-3197 (gay/straight, 5 rooms, Summer Rates Single $95–$125 Double $125–$175 Winter Rates Single $55–$75 Double $65–$125). Rooms at this property feature full amenities plus VCRs and private sitting areas. Also on-site is an eight-person Jacuzzi (where nudity is allowed), a small gym, billiards, and widescreen TV. Activities nearby include downhill skiing, horseback riding, golf, and tennis.

Campit   6635 118th Ave., Fennville, MI 49408; www.saugatuckweekends.com/campitvolunteers.htm 616-543-4335 or toll free 877-CAMPIT-1 (men and women, thirty campsites and forty-five RV hookups, call for rates). Campground open from May 1st to Oct. 31st.

Country Guest House   1673 38th St., Somerset, WI 54025; 715-247-3520 (mixed, 2 bedrooms, $75 and up). Located on twenty wooded acres in the St. Croix River Valley, this small guest house offers limited amenities but ample opportunity to enjoy the great outdoors.

Duckett House Inn & Farm   P.O. Box 441, Hot Springs, NC 28743; or 828-622-7621, www.bbonline.com/nc/ducketthouse/season.htm (mixed, 6 rooms, $43 and up). The rooms in this 1900 Victorian farmhouse, which is located on five wooded acres, feature fireplaces and ceiling fans; some have private baths. Activities include swimming in secluded swimming holes ("nudity is ok," they promise) and visiting Smokey Mountain National Park, one hour away.

Hateful Missy and Granny Butch's Boudoir & Manure Emporium   29 Jaramillo Loop, P.O. Box 556, Veguita, NM 87062;

800-397-2482 or 505-861-3328 (gay/lesbian, clothing optional, 4 rooms, $85–$125). This 4,100-square-foot, two-story adobe house lies on twelve acres in the Rio Grande river valley. Rooms feature color TV, VCR, cable, and "selected videos," as well as flowers and a fruit basket, a complimentary bottle of wine or cider, and "naughty candy on the pillows." Some bathrooms are attached to rooms, others are next door in the hall. An upstairs suite includes a king-sized bed and Jacuzzi. On the property is a pool table, and within a quarter mile are trails for walking, biking, and hiking. Pets are welcome with advance notice.

Hillside Campground P.O. Box 726, Binghamton, NY 13902; After March 1, call 727-869-6464, after April 570-756-2007, for your site reservation, or visit www.hillsidecampground.com (men & woman clothing optional, camping $30–$56; 4 cabins, $50/night, $180/weekend). This resort, located midway between Scranton, Pennsylvania, and Binghamton, New York, is open from the first weekend in May until the last weekend in September. Most campsites have electricity and water, and access to bath and shower facilities. Nudists have their own special area.

Jones' Pond Campground RD 1, Box 214, 9835 Old State Rd., Angelica, NY 14709; 716-567-8100 (men only, weekend rates: campsites, $26 first person, $24, each additional; Monday—Thursday: $10 first, $8 additional; 2 rental trailers that sleep four $60 + fees mentioned earlier). Located an hour and a half south of Rochester, this property is open from the first weekend in May to early October. Most sites have power and water hookups, and access to two bath units.

Maine-ly For You RR Box 745, Harrison, ME 04040; 207-782-2275 (gay and straight).

Ocean House 127 South Ocean Ave., Atlantic City, NJ 08401; 609-345-8203 (men only, 15 rooms, $34 and up). If you want the Atlantic City experience in a gay environment, this is one of the places to do it. This guest house used to be a convent, and now features a TV/VCR lounge, AC sun porch, and refrigerator. Includes morning coffee.

Rainbow Mountain Resort   210 Mt. Nebo Road, East Strouds-burg, PA 18301; 570-223-8484, www.rainbowmountain.com. Eighty-five-acre resort for men and women in the Pocono Mountains. Restaurant, dance club, lounge on property.

Rancho Cicada   P.O. Box 225, Plymouth, CA 95669; 209-245-4841, www.ranchocicadaretreat.com (mostly men in groups, 26 rooms, 2 cabin, campsites, call for rates). Located in the foothills of the Sierra Nevada Mountains, this property offers back-to-nature accommodations, although some rooms have TV and VCR, and the cabin has a refrigerator and fireplace. A hot tub and large deck are among the amenities, and nudity is allowed anywhere on the property.

Royal Palms Resort   2901 Terramar St., Ft. Lauderdale, FL 33304; 800-237-7256 or 954-564-6444, www.Royalpalms.com (gay/lesbian, 12 rooms and suites, $139–$289, including continental breakfast, complimentary beverages). Full amenities (except for some with shared baths) plus VCR, kitchenettes with refrigera-tors, and safer sex supplies. The property also features a pool and sun deck, where nudity is allowed. Also massage therapist available.

River's Edge   2311 Pulliam Mill Rd., Dewy Rose, GA 30634-7934; 706-213-8081 fax 706-213-6105 (mostly men, women wel-come, guest house, $25 and up; 30 campsites and 5 RV hookups, $12 and up). Cabins feature kitchens and bathrooms. Located near Atlanta, the property also features a pool and sun deck, where nudity is allowed, as well as hiking trails. www.camptheriversedge.com

Sallie & Eileen's Place   Box 409, Mendocino, CA 95460; 707-937-2028 (women only, 1 A-frame, $65, 1 cabin, $80, 2-night min-imum). The cabin features a queen-sized bed, double futon, and kitchen with refrigerators. Use of a hot tub, where nudity is allowed, is available for an additional charge.

Summit Lodge Resort   P.O. Box 951, Logan, OH 43138; 614-385-3521 or 614-385-6822 (mostly men, women welcome, cloth-ing optional, 15 rooms, $45 and up, camping sites). Summit Lodge features a pool, hot tub, sauna, and trails leading through secluded woods.

Surfside Resort Hotel   18 S. Mt. Vernon Ave., Atlantic City, NJ 08401; 609-347-0808 (men and women, 25 rooms, $45 and up weekdays, $65–$105 weekends, $105–$115 suite). Another way to see Atlantic City, right next to Studio Six, a gay dance club. Rooms feature bathrooms with hair dryers, TV, refrigerator, sun deck, and bar.

Swan Lake Bed and Breakfast   P.O. Box 1623, Jasper, FL 32052; 904-792-2771 (mixed gay/straight, 4 rooms, $25 and up; camping, $10). This property features limited amenities (it has shared baths), but offers a full breakfast and use of a hot tub.

Triangle Inn   P.O. Box 3235, Santa Fe, NM 87501; 850-973-8435; www.triangleinn.com. Each of the nine casitas, ranging from cozy studios to a large two-bedroom house, are decorated in southwestern style; continental breakfast is provided each day in your casita. Prices range from $60 to $140 in the winter and from $80 to $160 in the summer and during the winter holidays. Smoking and non-smoking rooms are available. The Inn is handicapped accessible and welcomes pets and children. A ranch with rooms that feature varying amenities, plus a hot tub, and a courtyard for sunbathing.

Wilderness Way Resort & Campground   P.O. Box 176, Wascott, WI 54890; 715-466-2635 (women only, 5 cabins, $48 and up, camping, $12 and up).

Wild Lily Ranch B&B   P.O. Box 313, Index, WA 98256; 360-793-2103; www.wildlilyranch.com (men and women, 99 percent gay, 3 cabins, $75/person + $10 each add'l, 2 fixed campsites, $45/couple). Three log cabins, constructed from cedar logs and cobblestone are open year-round. Plumbing is located in a detached bathhouse, which also features a Jacuzzi. During spring and summer, guests can also choose an established campsite, which is already set up with tent and raised beds— perfect for someone who may be a bit skittish about the rugged life. Continental breakfast is included with rates; nearby activities include whitewater rafting, skiing, and horseback riding.

6

ON YOUR OWN

**"Whenever possible, avoid airlines which
have anyone's first name in their titles, like
Bob's International Airline or Air Fred."**

—Miss Piggy, from *Miss Piggy's Guide to Life*
(as told to Henry Beard)

"We'd like to go to the train station, please." My boyfriend
Angel and I had just climbed into a cute little taxi in front of
our hotel in Prague. Our luggage was piled high on our laps.

The driver smiled and nodded, saying something in Czech
that neither Angel nor I understood. We pulled out into the
street and sped away.

After a few minutes of watching scenery go by, Angel turned
to me. "Isn't the train station back the other way?" It did seem
we were headed in the opposite direction.

"Excuse me," I called to the driver. Since I couldn't speak
Czech, I decided I should speak like Tarzan. "Train station that
way?!?" I pointed back the way we'd come.

The driver answered, in Czech, and kept driving. Eventually, we began passing neighborhoods that we recognized were nowhere near the station. We were also coming close to missing our train.

"No!" I said again. "That way!!" I made gigantic sweeping motions with my arms and torso. "Train station!!"

The man looked at us, apparently not understanding, and threw his hands up in the air. He kept driving.

"We want the train!" Angel and I both began making train noises. It was like some stupid commercial for travelers' checks or Coca-Cola.

We tried every word we knew associated with rail travel, but to no avail. He either didn't understand or didn't want to understand. Finally, Angel raised his hand and said the magic word: "Stop!"

The driver pulled over. We got out and found another taxi, which took us immediately to the train station, where we barely caught the last departure to Berlin.

All of this stress and confusion could have been avoided had we been traveling on an escorted tour. Then, even if there'd been a problem, the tour guide would have handled it for us.

But we honestly wouldn't give up all that stress and confusion for the world. It's part of the excitement of independent travel. I prefer the discomfort and inconvenience that comes with independent travel, because with the unpredictability of independent travel comes something else: *control*. I want to control my own schedule, and I *want* culture shock. I want to learn about people and places that are different from back home. Tours can be too soft and cushy; I don't want someone around making things easier; I want genuine travel experiences rather than a preplanned, guided excursion that only picks out the good stuff. I want the bad stuff, too.

Sure, independent travel is usually more work. There's no predetermined itinerary and no group leader to solve whatever problems that might come along. Even though using a travel agent can make planning independent travel much easier, when you're out on the road, you're still pretty much on your own.

But that's a big part of the attraction.

Here are some of the things that I like about independent travel:

• You have more control over your own schedule and activities. Group tours pick activities designed to please a group of people—not you as an individual. By traveling independently, you can tailor your itinerary to meet the specific needs and interests of you and your traveling companions.

• It's often cheaper than glamorous group tours, because you can select from a wider variety of accommodations and transportation options.

• You can meet more locals. Instead of hanging out with a bunch of Americans, you'll meet people from the region you're visiting, and, as a result, learn more about the local culture. (I don't travel all the way to France, for example, to meet people from New York City.) Thus, you'll learn a lot more about other cultures than if you were listening to some American tour guide reciting a memorized speech.

Best of all, planning your own vacation offers an infinite number of possibilities. This book offers but a few to get you started. I've also included some suggestions about destinations; you'll find more information in the "Classic Gay Destinations" chapter.

Don't think that independent travel completely shuts you out of the special offers and rates available from package deals. Several companies offer air and land vacations, but without an escort—in other words, you get a discounted rate, but don't have anyone planning your trip for you once you reach the destination. You're on your own to explore and have fun.

Of course, when traveling independently, you've obviously got to have a better handle on where you're going and what you're doing. A travel agent can be especially helpful in determining your course of action. The myriad of travel reference materials are invaluable, as well.

From the hundreds of gay people I've spoken with, it seems a lot of people enjoy traveling independently, at least for some trips. The general consensus is that there's a time and place for group travel *and* independent exploration.

THINGS TO THINK ABOUT FIRST   What kind of travel do you like?
What kinds of activities and attractions interest you most? Are
tours available that address your interests, or are you better
off tailoring something to suit your needs? Do you like group
activities, or prefer to be just with people you already know?
Do you have access to travel guides, tourism boards, and other
sources of information that can help you make travel plans?

QUESTIONS TO ASK THE TRAVEL PROVIDER   What is the price
range for airfare and accommodations in the chosen destination? (If it's important to you) Are there specific areas where
lesbians and gay men can meet? Is there any organization that
offers means to meet other travelers or locals? What kind of
ground transportation is available?

Independent Travel Packages

It is possible to get the discounts associated with group travel,
without the escorts and preset schedules.

Unescorted travel packages include air transportation,
accommodations, and perhaps a rental car and discounts on
other products. The packages are well-established in the mainstream travel industry (one look at the Sunday paper's travel
section will confirm that).

If there is no escort and no tour, what makes a travel package gay or lesbian? First of all, they feature gay-popular destinations. Second, the mainstream transportation companies and
hotels or resorts involved in the package have already "proven"
their gay-friendliness and should be more likely to show sensitivity to your needs (in other words, the hotel won't cringe
when you ask for a double bed for you and your lover).

In recent years, some companies—including major mainstream suppliers like American Airlines and major gay operators like RSVP—have attempted to market independent gay
travel packages, but so far these efforts have not panned out. In
the meantime, you can use your own smarts (along with those
of your travel agent and resources in the bookstore, library and
Internet) to determine what packages and destinations are best
for you.

The Frequent Flyer Dream Vacation

"Going to Asia is something we've always wanted to do, and this seemed the best way to do it," says Roger Timmons. He and his boyfriend, Ted Lorenzo, took a trip to Hong Kong and Singapore for free, using frequent flyer miles.

Just about everyone is a member of some frequent flyer program. But most people don't end up with free tickets worth over $1,500. With a little strategizing, though, you can find yourself flying cheaper or even free on a 747 bound for destinations on the other side of the world.

Shop around before deciding on a program. Getting the awards you want depends on those maddening airline rules and regulations, and it can be even more frustrating if your airline won't let you transfer or share awards with your lover. Check to make sure your program allows transferring of awards to anyone, e.g., domestic partners, boyfriends, girlfriends, etc.

Beyond that, getting one of those big awards is about the same, regardless of who you sleep with. It starts with planning. "Neither of us travel a whole lot, just a few times a year on business for vacations," explains Roger. "So we concentrated on flying as much as we could with one carrier, US Airways, because that airline's mileage never expires." Most airlines now offer mileage that won't expire as long as you keep the account active (by accruing miles at least once every three years, either by flying, using a credit card or other program-linked service). Mileage that never dies can be a blessing for infrequent frequent flyers.

Roger also linked up their long-distance phone service with his frequent flyer account, and both men took out credit cards that earned them mileage, too. After a year and half of regular traveling and using these other services, they'd both accumulated over 90,000 miles—which was enough, with a special offer from US Airways, to get two business-class tickets to Asia. They decided to fly into Bangkok and return from Hong Kong. "Both cities were places we'd always been interested in, and so it was worth it to pay for a cheap ticket between the two," Roger explains.

Roger and Ted called nearly five months ahead of time to reserve their seats—which is not a bad idea, given how difficult it can be to claim frequent flyer awards. Once they were all set with air, they used their local travel agent to make arrangements for hotels, ground transportation, and travel between the two cities. With the transpacific ticket taken care of, they had plenty of money to use in Asia. "It was culturally enriching, and a lot of fun, too," says Roger. "Flying on a frequent flyer award is a really satisfying experience, especially when you're traveling such a long way. Finally, all of your traveling pays off and you can do something you enjoy—for free."

THINGS TO THINK ABOUT FIRST   How often do you travel and how quickly would you plan on reaching an award level? Is the award you want available from the airline you fly most, or should you review your choice of air carriers? Can you use other methods to get mileage, such as credit cards, dining programs, etc.?

QUESTIONS TO ASK THE TRAVEL PROVIDER   Can my frequent flyer mileage expire? Who can I transfer awards to? Who can I claim as a companion for award travel? What are the rules regarding mileage inheritance in case of death?

Airlines and Frequent Flyer Programs

Sure, an airline seat is uncomfortable no matter what airline. But don't be fooled into thinking that all airlines are the same (or that any of them are perfect). Some carriers have made great strides in improving their relations with lesbian and gay travelers, while others are still at the gate.

The major area in which airlines differ is in their recognition of same-sex couples. How they view our relationships results in several policies that affect us as travelers: frequent flyer programs, bereavement fares, and other peripherals like membership perks in airline clubs and eligibility for some special fares.

Frequent flyer programs were the first area to see improvement, because people complained the most about it. After numerous lawsuits, the airlines realized that it was easier to relax the rules and allow frequent flyers to transfer or share awards with just about anyone. Still, there are some restrictions with some airlines on some awards—so you'd be wise to ask about transferability (and read the fine print) with any program before building up miles with any one program.

You should also check the rules regarding frequent flyer account inheritance. Considering how valuable mileage is, including yours in your will isn't a bad idea. But can you leave miles to your lover? Keep in mind that an airline that already recognizes spousal status in airline clubs or frequent flyer programs is less likely to give you problems later.

The same goes for bereavement fares, which offer discounts of 15 to 50 percent off the standard fare, for travel after the death of a close relative. Requirements vary widely and are subject to change, so shop around.

It would be wonderful if every airline had started treating us as equals by the time you read this book. Since that is unlikely, the following summary can serve as a guide to some of the airlines that have taken steps to treat gay and lesbian passengers better. These carriers are likely to continue addressing our needs:

American Airlines has responded to past negative publicity in a positive way. In the early 1990s, the carrier's problems were many. It was sued by an AIDS patient who was removed from one of its flights. The carrier also received low marks when an attendant on a flight returning from the 1993 March on Washington requested the plane's blankets and pillows be changed to protect everyone from AIDS. And employees have accused American of responding too slowly to antigay graffiti and refusing to let gay flight attendants work some charter flights.

In response, American has taken a leadership role in the industry, instituting gay- and AIDS-sensitivity training for all its employees, and a nondiscrimination clause to protect the homosexuals in its workforce. The airline frequently sponsors gay events across the country, and it was the first airline to create a position for a gay marketing manager. American's

Admirals Club offers spousal membership discounts to domestic partners. In 1996, American became the first major carrier to work with tour operators (**RSVP** and **Gogo Worldwide Vacations**) to offer gay-specific, air-inclusive tour packages, under the name **Plaanet RSVP** (the program, however, has been discontinued). American also allows frequent flyers to will their mileage to anyone they choose.

Cape Air, a tiny carrier that specializes in flights to the very-gay cape of Massachusetts and to even gayer Key West, recognizes its gay clientele through print ads, and is a presence at gay travel expos.

Continental Airlines has received high marks for the attention it pays to the lesbian and gay community. They've sponsored several gay events (including the massive Gay Games IV in New York City), although they have yet to introduce a specific gay marketing plan.

Lufthansa, the largest German carrier, has begun building its presence through gay travel expos, and gay-specific packages.

Northwest Airlines had indicated interest in developing a comprehensive gay marketing program, but has yet to do so. So far, they've included discount coupons through advertising in several gay publications.

Qantas, the Australian airline, has participated in gay travel functions and packages, and is expected to become more aggressive in attracting gay and lesbian travelers.

Virgin Atlantic Airways is a real history maker. Not only does it advertise regularly in gay publications, it was the first airline to offer vacation packages specifically for gay travelers (unfortunately, they were later discontinued, although the airline continues to market its mainstream packages to gay markets). Virgin is sisters with Heaven, one of London's most popular gay discos. How many airlines can you say that about?

Like most companies, airlines usually don't change unless they're prodded. If you encounter unfair rules or just plain homophobia with any carrier, let them know. Complain. Even consider taking them to court, because that's what recently prompted important changes in frequent flyer programs.

And when you fly, consider the following: Has the airline demonstrated its commitment to our community by advertising, sponsoring gay events, and establishing guidelines that treat us as equals? Does the airline deserve your money?

The Perfect Gay Road Trip—All the Essentials

As much as we focus on the fast life and jet-setting about the globe, there's a lot to be said for a good old-fashioned road trip. Driving the open highways of America, we can get in touch with our roots, cement our friendships, and get on people's nerves in the confined spaces of a small car for days on end.

I've always found political rallies—especially in Washington, D.C.—to be a great excuse to load up the car. But if you're planning a gay road trip, it doesn't really matter where you're going, as long as you have a good time getting there.

The most important thing is that you have the right attitude and the right people going with you. What fun would the film *Priscilla, Queen of the Desert* have been if those three guys didn't look good in women's clothing? And would the two straight women in *Boys on the Side* have had any fun if Whoopi Goldberg hadn't been there to play a lesbian?

Herewith, a suggested list of stuff to bring on your perfect gay road trip:

A road map. Whoever is in the front passenger seat is designated the navigator, and must read, loudly and with force, all necessary driving directions from the map. During lapses in conversation, the navigator can also read aloud each road sign that the car passes.

Symbols to identify your car as a homovehicle. Slap on those pink triangles, rainbow flags, or whatever it takes. It's a great feeling to get a friendly toot from other motorists, and most of the people who'd rather see you dead are too stupid to know what the symbols mean.

Wigs and other costumes. Put them on just before you get to a tollbooth and speak in very deep voices. It will confuse and delight the tollbooth clerks.

A trusty gay and lesbian travel guide. The one in your hands is a great one to start with, of course, but don't be shy about buying or borrowing one of the excellent books out there that highlight gay hot spots on a city-by-city basis. Then, no matter where you wind up, you'll be able to track down gay-friendly accommodations, bars, and community centers.

Music that everyone likes. Suggested tracks include a choice of gay and lesbian classics. Take turns playing D.J., since your own music is sure to bother the other passengers at some point. Feel free to argue about whose music is better.

Personal stereo system with headphones. For times when the music everyone else wants to hear is no good and you're sick of listening to the constant whining of your travel companions.

Munchies and drinks. No booze, of course—but perhaps some sparkling cider and plastic champage flutes, to toast every time you cross a state line. In addition, Little Debbie's line of quality snack products provides affordable yet enjoyable sugar rushes to help you go the extra mile.

Maalox and Pepto-Bismol. For after the munchies and drinks.

Blank sheets of paper and a magic marker. You can use these to write notes to other motorists, such as "You have a flat" or "You're cute" or "Meet me at exit 47."

A vanity mirror. You have to look good when you arrive.

A sense of humor. Nobody wants to ride with a grump.

Campy Destinations

The strong connection between gay people—men in particular—and camp may never be satisfactorily explained. Whether it's nature or nurture, our community has developed a keen appreciation for things that are so bad, they're good.

This sense of style sometimes extends to our travel plans; usually not as the only objective, but as an important aspect of a successful vacation. In any U.S. city with a large gay population, it's easy to find stores and sites that are tributes to the importance of kitsch in our lives.

It's surprising the amount of campy tourist sites located all over this great land of ours. You could plan a cross-country venture and come across something weird every day of your trip. While gay culture may center around large urban areas, you'll find that a good deal of what inspires us is actually from small-town America, just like many of us once were.

There have been several good books that highlight such pieces of Americana; *Roadside America* and *TVacations* are among the best for planning your tacky travels.

In the name of public interest and developing U.S. tourism, I've put together a list of some of America's great campy tourist sites, with special emphasis on things that are important to us as a community (is it any surprise that actresses rank high on this list?). You'll see that many of the most exciting sites are located just a little off the beaten path.

The Top Campy Destinations in the United States

Ava Gardner Museum   Smithfield, NC; 919-934-5830, www. avagardner.org. Two dollars gets you into the house in which this sultry screen star was raised. Filled with memorabilia from her life and movies. Afterward, you may want to visit nearby Sunset Memorial Park, where she's buried.

Cheryl Ladd Room   Huron, SD; 605-352-9238. Fans of *Charlie's Angels* (meaning a lot of gay men over age 30) should make a pilgrimage to this special room dedicated to Farrah Fawcett's replacement, located in a restaurant called The Barn. Ladd worked here before moving west to pursue her Hollywood dream. And look how far she's come.

Dollywood   Pigeon Forge, TN; 615-428-9488, www.dolly wood.com. The Christian musical numbers staged in this amusement park may be a bit disconcerting, and the roller coaster may make you a bit queasy, but it's all part of the experience at the park bearing Dolly Parton's name.

Graceland   Memphis, TN; 901-332-3322, www.elvis.com/ graceland. Gay and straight travelers alike just can't get enough of the King's over-the-top estate. Who says only gay men can do interior decorating?

Houmas House   Burnside, LA; 888-323-8314 or 225-473-7841, www.houmashouse.com. If you've seen the campy movie *Hush . . . Hush, Sweet Charlotte,* you won't want to miss this gorgeous antebellum plantation house where Bette Davis slowly went crazy.

The Judy Garland Museum   Grand Rapids, MN; 800-664-JUDY, www.judygarlandmuseum.com. One of the original divas. Judy's parents operated a vaudeville house in this town for a while, and you can relive some of Judy's greatest moments here.

Liberace Museum   Las Vegas, NV; 702-798-5595, www.liberace.org. Share the space with groups of older straight women who come to marvel at the spectacularly ostentatious taste of this musical marvel.

Mall of America   Bloomington, MN; 612-883-8800, www.mallofamerica.com. Shop 'til you drop at the nation's largest mall. A tribute to the importance of suburban shopping centers, this monstrosity offers hundreds of stores and its own indoor amusement park.

The Mary Tyler Moore House   Franklin Ave. at Lake of the Isles, Minneapolis, MN; no phone. After you spend all your money at the Mall of America, head over here. You can't even go inside (it's a private home), and it's been repainted so you almost won't recognize it. But no trip to Minnesota would be complete without making the pilgrimage here, and perhaps throwing your hat up in the air (à la Mary) for a quick photo.

National Cowgirl Museum and Hall of Fame   Fort Worth, TX; 817-336-4475, www.cowgirl.net. Women made plenty of contributions to the Old West, and Hereford's the place to commemorate it. Begun in 1975 in the town of Hereford, the museum was preparing to open an expanded facility as this book went to press.

Southfork Ranch Event and Conference Center   Parker, TX; 972-442-7800, www.southfork.com. If you were a fan of the hit TV series *Dallas,* you won't want to miss this museum, located inside the ranch that served as J.R.'s TV home for nearly ten years. You'll be amazed at Sue Ellen's gown, and gaze in awe at Jock's will.

South of the Border   Dillon, SC; 800-845-6011 or 843-774-2411, www.pedroland.com. Imagine enjoying the view from the top of a gigantic sombrero. It's the kitschy, gringo version of Mexico, complete with its own motel and campground. Stay a few days and "sleep weeth Pedro," urges the Website.

Finding the Perfect Place to Stay (No Matter Where You're Going)

I'll never forget the time my boyfriend and I checked into a large chain motel along a highway in Massachusetts.

Angel and I entered the lobby and I asked for a room. The clerk didn't miss a beat as she checked her computer. "A room with two beds . . . one moment please."

"No, actually, one is just fine," I said.

The woman looked a bit dazed, but continued checking her computer. After another minute, she looked up. "*How many beds do you want?*"

"One, please."

She continued computing, but finally looked up again, totally confused. "You want two beds?"

Any wonder why hotels need to provide employees with sensitivity training?

Hotel and motel chains lag behind other travel businesses in terms of meeting the needs of gays and lesbians. In the early 1990s, the American Hotel and Motel Association implemented a sensitivity training program for its employees, which addressed cultural diversity in the workplace and included information about homosexual employees. But the program only addressed relations with coworkers. So far, there has been no large-scale program to teach heterosexual hotel employees how to accept the fact that gays and lesbians like to share beds with their lovers.

This is just one of the challenges in finding a pleasant place to stay. Accommodations serve different purposes for different people, depending on your personal preferences and the kind of vacation you're planning. You may be happy with nothing more than a cheap, simple place to hang your hat after an exciting day of sight-seeing. Or you may be looking for an elegant, full-service hotel to pamper you and cater to your every need. You may be looking to get lucky without having to set foot outside the hotel. Or maybe you want a cozy place where you and your lover can hold hands without being stared at.

Large lodging chains, especially in the United States, are more likely to offer the convenience of size, plus a toll-free reservation number, tie-ins with frequent flyer programs, and what I call the "McDonald's Advantage"; namely, you always know what to expect, because they generally offer uniformity of accommodations, rates, quality, and convenience. It's also easy to find a mainstream chain near popular tourist spots.

At larger hotels, of course, if you're traveling with a lover, you run the risk that they won't understand why you want a queen-sized bed (and in many parts of the world, you probably couldn't get a double bed even if you were heterosexual).

Mainstream hotels are also less likely to be understanding if you bring a newfound "friend" home for the evening, although the larger properties may be so big they don't even notice who's going up to your room.

Even at mainstream hotels, concierges should be able and willing to help you with any "gay-specific" local information. If they can't or won't, they're not doing their job.

If you're not sure how gay-sensitive a particular hotel is, you can always call the hotel directly, ask to speak with a manager, and inquire about their gay sensitivity. Sure, it's pretty direct, but you can do it. Ask the same questions that we gay travel writers ask. "Do you welcome gay guests? Is the staff trained to be sensitive to the needs of gay and lesbian travelers? Would I have any problems getting one bed to share with my partner?" You may find a few surprised hotel managers when you make these calls, but you may also be pleasantly surprised with how savvy some hotels are.

Joie de Vivre Hotels, a collection of boutique hotels and B&Bs in San Francisco, is a great example of how a company can capture the mainstream *and* gay markets. The company actively markets to gay and lesbian travelers and extends a warm welcome to us at its hip properties like the Hotel Rex at Union Square. In addition to mainstream ads and brochures, gay-specific materials speak our language: "Our staff will give you information on the hippest gay hangouts, happenings and hot spots," promises one brochure. "Just tell us what's on the agenda and we'll fill your dance card quicker than you can say 'To Wong Foo!' "

If you're not getting the service you deserve, wield those all-powerful weapons: the pen and the dollar. Write to the company's headquarters whenever you have an unpleasant experience, and don't patronize a place that's given you a bad experience.

Resources

Joie de Vivre Hotels, 800-738-7477, www.jdvhotels.com

How to Save Money on a Room

No matter what kind of accommodations you're looking for, it pays to shop around for the best deal possible. Some basic tips:

• When a hotel reservations agent or your travel agent gives you a rate, always ask if there is a lower rate available. Frequently, there are weekend specials and discounts available that they may not mention at first. Even if you're planning to stay at a super-luxurious place, make it clear that you are looking for the lowest rate for those accommodations. You may be eligible for discount rates that are offered to senior citizens, AAA members, and corporate travelers.

• Make reservations as far in advance as you can, and if you can, call the individual property directly, rather than a toll-free number. The people at the hotel itself have more knowledge about individual specials and have more authority to be flexible.

• Pay attention to your frequent flyer account mailings for special deals available only to members of the program. Also, make sure you get mileage for any stays at properties that participate in your mileage program. And don't forget that some frequent flyer awards programs include free hotel stays.

Gay Hotels and Bed & Breakfasts

The best gay hotels and bed and breakfasts provide wonderful experiences for travelers. These properties boast picturesque, sometimes historically significant accommodations in beautiful residential neighborhoods, conveniently close to sight-seeing, shopping, and gay life. They may be located in tiny towns or in a lush, peaceful countryside. The proprietors are often enthusiastic local experts, always ready to point you in the direction of the best restaurants, tourist sights, or clubs.

But not all B&Bs are created equal. Don't assume that a B&B is acceptable just because it's listed in a gay guide. The truth is, some of them charge ridiculous prices for substandard facilities.

So be careful before you choose. Positive reviews from friends who've already been there are the best way to pick a B&B. But if personal referrals are not available, check with your travel agent or do research in travel guides—the gay ones have lots of listings, but the listings that don't accept advertising will be much more objective in their write-ups. A nongay reservation service, Bed & Breakfast Network (212-645-8134), can direct you to some mainstream establishments. Most importantly, call the property with questions, and only make a reservation if you're satisfied with the answers.

THINGS TO THINK ABOUT FIRST   What kind of an environment do you prefer—all-male, all-female, gay and lesbian, mixed gay/straight? Is it important to be near all the action, or are you more interested in finding a quiet, attractive neighborhood to relax? What is your price range? What amenities do you need, and which are you willing to forego?

QUESTIONS TO ASK THE TRAVEL PROVIDER   Is the property all-gay? Men/women? How would you describe the atmosphere (e.g., clothing optional)? How big are the bedrooms? Do they have a television/telephone? Are there private bathrooms, and if so, does it cost extra to get a room with one? Is breakfast or any other meals included? What amenities—like a sunroof, pool, restaurant, bar—are on the premises? What is the neighborhood like, and what attractions are close by? Do you accept credit card payment? Until what time will you hold a reservation? If money is an issue, be sure to ask for the cheapest room available, because the first price quoted may be for a more expensive room.

Home Exchanges

Location is everything when it comes to accommodations, and sometimes the best way to stay in the middle of everything, and to save money as a result, is to participate in a home exchange. With this setup, you have full use of someone's home—sometimes a house, sometimes an apartment—in exchange for their using yours. You can feasibly use exchanges to arrange accommodations just about anywhere in the world; it is most common, however, for people traveling to Europe or elsewhere in North America.

Home exchange agencies charge a fee for setting this up, usually starting under $100. It's recommended that you plan at least a year in advance. But you must be very careful about the details of the exchange. Make sure you know exactly what kind of place you're going to be staying in (location, facilities, size of space), as well as what sort of people will be staying in *your* home.

The mainstream agencies should also be able to provide you with adequate service—just don't expect them to know where the gay ghettos are in every city.

The only specifically gay home exchange is **Mi Casa Su Casa,** an Oakland, California-based company. To participate, you pay a $78 annual membership fee, and complete an application form with information about your house or apartment. After sending in the fee, application, and a photograph of your home, your listing appears in subsequent editions of the company's membership journal, which is published every spring and fall. You'll then be able to browse through the guide and contact people whose homes interest you. Also available are room exchanges, in case you share your home or apartment with other people but want to exchange your bedroom for one in another city or country.

Mi Casa Su Casa currently has active members in twenty-one states and twenty-one countries, including Brazil, Canada, Mexico, New Zealand, and various destinations in Asia, the Caribbean, and Europe.

Resources:

Note: With the exception of Mi Casa Su Casa, all the following are mainstream home exchange agencies. They should be able to help you find a place in your desired destination, but don't expect them to know all the details about the latest gay hot spots.

American-International Homestays, 800-876-2048 (Europe, Russia, China), www.aihtravel.com/homestays

Citizens Exchange Council, 212-643-1985 (Europe, Russia)

Friendship Force, 404-522-0596 (Europe), www.friendship-force.org

Mi Casa Su Casa, 800-215-2272, www.gayhometrade.com

Servas, 212-267-0252 (U.S. and other countries worldwide), www.usservas.org

Traveling Safely

I was having a wonderful time in Buenos Aires, hitting all the tourist sites, taking lots of photographs, and visiting several of the popular gay discos.

I was in a great mood as I was walking back to my hotel after a full day of touring. Suddenly, I felt something cold and wet against the back of my neck. I turned around and saw a man and a woman, who had one hand full of an ice cream cone and the other full of napkins.

"Oh, I'm so sorry!" she said. "Let me help clean you up!"

She handed the ice cream to her companion and approached me with the napkins, rubbing the back of my neck furiously, as I tried to tell her I could clean myself up.

"Why don't you let my friend hold your backpack so I can clean the back of your shirt?" she asked.

Bingo. They were trying to rip me off. I may have looked like an idiotic tourist, but I was not about to have her "friend" run off with my bag, leaving me with nothing but ice cream. This was one of the oldest tricks in the book (sometimes it's done with ketchup or mustard), and one of the many cons that travelers, gay or straight, must look out for.

Cities like New York, Miami, and Rio de Janeiro may get all the bad publicity, but the fact is that you have to take precautions wherever you go, especially when traveling abroad. Following are some universal safety tips:

• Photocopy all important documents, including your passport, and keep a list of your traveling papers with the numbers of your travelers' checks.

• Find out the location of the U.S. consulate or embassy before you get to your destination. They can help you out in an emergency.

• Don't wear flashy jewelry or expensive watches in public. It's an invitation to thieves.

• Don't carry money, credit cards, tickets, and other valuables all in the same place. Avoid using back pockets, because those are most susceptible to pickpockets.

• Try not to stand out as overly touristy. Carry a local newspaper under your arm, even if you can't read the language. Dress like a local, if that's possible.

• Don't look at large tourist maps and brochures in public. Plan your routes and mode of transport before you leave your hotel. If you must, keep a small map or list of directions that will fit in the palm of your hand.

• Don't automatically trust someone who offers to help you.

• If someone approaches you in public and begins asking you detailed questions about where you're staying, where you're going, etc., be as vague as possible. Don't give out specific room numbers. You can even say that you are visiting a friend so they can't tell that you're new to the area.

• At night, stay in well-populated, well-lit areas.

• When you leave your hotel room, leave a light on and a radio playing softly.

• Don't leave valuables on the beach, unless it is a protected, private area.

• Don't wear clothing with a military or governmental theme, such as army fatigues or camouflage.

• Trust your instincts: if something doesn't seem right, it probably isn't.

Special Precautions for Gay and Lesbian Travelers

Given the prevailing attitudes toward homosexuality in many parts of the world, safety is an especially important concern for us. We're sometimes susceptible to danger and discrimination that other travelers don't even think about.

Even though many of us experience a level of comfort in our hometowns or in the major gay destinations, the rest of the world is not always as welcoming. Keep this in mind during your trip. It may be a good idea not to wear that safe sex T-shirt immediately upon arriving in a place you're not familiar with. Once you've got a feel for the region, then you can begin making political statements. Be especially cautious when traveling abroad, however, because it can take a lot longer to assess the state of gay and lesbian life in other countries.

Following are some general safety tips especially for us:

• Carry a whistle and blow it if someone gives you trouble.

• If you're planning on visiting a bar or club, locate it first during daylight hours. That way, you'll know it still exists and also be more sure of your route at night, when it's less safe to get lost.

• When visiting clubs and bars, it's not a bad idea to keep an eye on your open bottle of beer or beverage glass. Occasionally, people will slip drugs into the drinks of unwitting clubgoers and then take their belongings while they're passed out.

• Don't bring someone you don't know home with you, unless you've introduced them to your friends. If you can't do that, make your new friend register at your hotel.

• If you have any problems, report it to the local gay hotline or antiviolence project, if there is one.

And a few tips specifically for gay men:

• When traveling in some parts of the United States and the world, it may be tempting for gay men to talk to hustlers and prostitutes. But keep in mind that these men are often not gay, and are in it for one reason: money. This doesn't mean that there are no hustlers with hearts of gold—many of these men are trying to make money in an honest, albeit illegal way (it is the oldest profession in the world, though). But you should be aware of the realities of the situation and not fool yourself into blindly trusting a professional hustler. They can sometimes take advantage of their clients, and tourists are a prime target.

• Use extreme caution if you decide to actually "interact" with a hustler. It's best not to bring someone you've just met back to your own room, unless you're staying at a hotel where he will have to register with the front desk. Otherwise, find another hotel room. But don't follow the guy anywhere that you are unfamiliar with or don't feel comfortable with. If there is to be a financial arrangement, work out the details ahead of time to prevent misunderstandings and potential arguments later.

General Discrimination

Once, as I was riding a late-night bus across Chile, I fell asleep with my head on my male friend's shoulder. Perfectly innocent, right? Imagine my surprise when the bus attendant woke me up and asked us to sit in separate seats.

"You are offending the other passengers," he charged.

That pissed me off. We deal with crap like that way too often, everywhere in the world. But we moved.

Sometimes, you don't have much choice. In the case of the Chilean bus, we changed seats rather than get into an argument that would potentially dump us off in the middle of the Atacama Desert.

But often, you have more power than you might realize. You're a consumer and deserve the same kind of treatment as any other traveler. Within the United States, local laws regarding discrimination may even provide you with a legal case; check with the local gay switchboard for organizations that can help you.

Even in places that don't have laws to protect your rights, you can still fight back. Ask to speak to a manager or supervisor. Threaten to not spend money on the company's products or services. Or go along with the scum who did you wrong, but then write a letter to the customer relations department of the company. Be detailed in describing what happened, and that you will not stand for it. You can even request specific compensation for your negative experience, whether it be vouchers for free travel or hotel stays, or frequent flyer bonuses.

Complaining can work wonders for your self-esteem, and even for gay rights!

How to Find Gay Culture (Almost) Anywhere

Looking for gay life in New York or Los Angeles is child's play. Even if you've never been there before, you'll find the gay ghettos in no time. But what about the millions of destinations where gay life isn't so obvious?

Some form of gay and lesbian life exists everywhere, and you can track it down with a bit of luck and common sense. So even if you're sent away on a sudden business trip, you won't have to eat every meal at Houlihan's, watching baseball on a big-screen TV.

Of course, the techniques may differ a bit, depending on whether you're embarking on a far-reaching cultural tour of foreign lands, or just taking a quick hop to Straightsville, U.S.A.

Before Leaving

Look in every gay travel guide you can get your hands on. Many destinations are only listed in a few guides, so check your local bookstore or order resources by mail (try A Different Light at 888-343-4002, www.adifferentlightbookstore.com). Photocopy the appropriate pages, so you won't have to lug around a heavy world travel guide during your trip. Don't forget to look at mainstream guides, too, because some of them now list information on gay culture (this proved a lifesaver to me during a visit to Hong Kong, when all my gay guides were severely outdated and I found myself trapped in clubs with puking straight people one night).

Surf the Internet. The World Wide Web is an amazing source of information about destinations worldwide. You can start with something as simple as a search for the word "gay" plus the name of the place you're going—in some cases this will bring up more information than you could possible sort through; for destinations with a less-developed gay and lesbian scene, it may bring up next to nothing.

You can also try starting at some specific gay and lesbian Web sites that may have information. Here are some of my favorites:

www.damron.com: Damron features a good number of links for tour operators and specific events worldwide.

www.gayjet.com: GayJet is an online-travel service that also provides destination and tour information. Operated by Community Marketing, a San Francisco-based travel marketing company.

www.iglhrc.org: The International Gay & Lesbian Human Rights Commission offers information about local gay and lesbian rights issues and organizations around the world.

www.iglta.org: The International Gay & Lesbian Travel Association has links to a few tour operators.

www.outandabout.com: The online version of the popular gay and lesbian travel newsletter, Out and About has a great catalog of detailed destination information from its back issues, although if you're not a subscriber you'll have to pay to access it.

www.pinkpassport.com: A British-based Web site with global listings.

www.planetout.com: This popular Web site has useful listings for the world's most popular gay and lesbian travel destinations.

www.qtmagazine.com: QT Magazine has feature articles and some listings for various international and domestic destinations.

www.purpleroofs.com: A helpful Web site listing gay and gay-friendly accommodations (many small properties and guest houses) around the world. A good source for inexpensive lodging ideas for the independent traveler.

www.roadsideamerica.com: This is not a gay or lesbian Web site, but it's a great source for information about offbeat—often hilarious—tourist attractions throughout the United States. Whether it's the Zippo Lighter Visitors Center, the Hall of Criminals, or the burial place of your favorite animal star, this is the place to look.

If you can, book in a hotel that's gay or gay-friendly. These hotels should be listed in gay guides. Even if the hotel is not exclusively gay, the people there may be a source of information after your arrival.

Contact local gay groups ahead of time. If you find listings for gay organizations that are located at your destination, contact them. Tell them your dates of travel and that you're interested in connecting with the local gay and lesbian community. They can provide you with information.

Tell all your friends where you're going. Once the word gets out, you might find a friend of a friend who's been there, too.

If you've tried everything and can't find a trace of a gay community, try contacting organizations or people *near* your destination. When I couldn't find anything gay listed for a trip to La Paz, Bolivia, I started contacting organizations in Lima, Peru, who graciously got back to me with contact names in La Paz.

After Arriving

Look up the word "gay," "lesbian," or "homo" in the phone book. (That is, if the language spoken bears any similarity to

English—the word "gay" has been accepted into an impressive number of languages worldwide.) Sometimes tracking down homo culture can be as simple as looking it up in a phone book. Then you can call the local gay switchboard or visit gay bookstores.

Visit the traditional gay hunting grounds. For at least the past century or two, homosexuals have been attracted to parks, museums, commercial centers, community centers, and beaches. Guides to foreign countries may be woefully outdated regarding gay businesses, but cruising areas don't change as rapidly. Visit the areas listed—not just for cruising, but because, sometimes, you can actually meet helpful people.

Ask the hotel concierge, local tourism office, or even taxi drivers. Sure, there might be some places where this is ill-advised due to rampant homophobia, but you could be pleasantly surprised how helpful straight locals can sometimes be. In tourism-heavy areas, for example, concierges and taxi drivers make their tips from being able to provide services and information to tourists. Why shouldn't they be willing to tell you where the nearest gay or lesbian bar is? It's in their own best interest to keep the customer satisfied.

Getting in the Mood—Movies and Books to Prepare You for Travel

Guidebooks are essential for vacation planning, especially when you're traveling independently. But they don't provide the depth of the travel experience. Movies and books can help introduce you to the culture, history, and characteristics of a destination, or maybe just put you in the mood to travel, regardless of where you're going.

Keep in mind that this is a very brief, very selective list of some of the most popular, gayest works out there. A visit to your library, bookstore, or video store will produce a multitude of other works that can help create a sense of place and make your vacation richer and more rewarding. For extensive listings of books, check *The Traveler's Reading Guide* by Maggy Simony.

Books

Cracks in the Iron Closet by David Tuller. Tuller's travels through gay and lesbian Russia makes for great social commentary and travel essay.

Faggots by Larry Kramer. This riveting novel dives into the decadent lifestyle of Fire Island and Manhattan before the AIDS crisis, and finds it to be rather empty.

Gay New York by George Chauncey. A highly readable history of gay life in New York City.

Giovanni's Room by James Baldwin. A heartbreaking look at gay life in the Paris of yesteryear.

Tales of the City by Armistead Maupin. The interwoven lives of San Franciscans gay and straight through the years shows the breadth of this city's communities and experiences.

Movies

The Adventures of Priscilla, Queen of the Desert (1994): The quintessential gay road-trip film, although most people probably couldn't afford so many costume changes.

Airport (1970), *Airport 1975* (1974), *Airport '77* (1977), *The Concorde: Airport '79* (1979): These films forever linked Karen Black, Helen Hayes, and George Kennedy to air travel. Fabulous, over-the-top camp.

Lie Down With Dogs: What's life like for a gay man in Provincetown? Rent this movie for a lighthearted look.

If It's Tuesday, This Must Be Belgium (1969). The quintessential European whirlwind tour.

The Out-of-Towners (1970): Jack Lemmon and Sandy Dennis star in this grating yet enjoyable film about everything that can possibly go wrong to a pair of uptight travelers.

Paris is Burning (1990): You may have seen Madonna's "Vogue" video five thousand times, but you won't really understand the New York City subculture that it was riding off of until you see this winning documentary.

The Poseidon Adventure (1972): Okay, so maybe it won't really get you in the mood for a cruise, but it's such a good film!

Sunset Boulevard. (1950): A masterpiece of macabre humor that portrays the downside of Hollywood's star machine.

Thelma and Louise (1991): Now this is the way to travel: in a classic car, with the cops at your tail, gorgeous scenery in front of you, and your best friend by your side.

To Wong Foo, Thanks for Everything, Julie Newmar (1995): Silly and harmless (and not a great film), this movie may still inspire you to hit the road and redecorate every town you come across.

The Joys of Using Gay-Friendly Businesses— Rental Car Companies

Would your parents rent a car from a company that refused to recognize their marriage and then charged them more money as a result?

That's what happens to gay and lesbian travelers every day.

The bottom line: If you're not supporting gay-friendly travel companies, you may be spending more money than you should, and you may not be treated fairly.

When airlines and rent-a-car companies set up corporate guidelines, they have a choice. In the old days (all of five years ago), they all chose to ignore the gay and lesbian market, especially our long-term relationships, in order to make more money in the short term. Today, several companies have decided it's more cost-effective to cultivate our loyalty by treating us as equals. So now we have a choice.

At first glance, mainstream travel companies may all look the same. But they differ in how they treat gay and lesbian customers. We're not talking about isolated incidents of a ticket agent screaming "faggot," we're talking about subtle, yet official corporate policies that dictate whether or not we receive the same service as our straight friends.

These policies tend to affect gay couples more than singles, because married heterosexuals almost always receive some sort of break from frequent flyer programs, rental car companies, and other travel businesses. Only recently have some of these benefits become available to homosexual couples who can prove the equivalent of spousal status.

How do you prove it? It depends. Some companies simply require identification from each partner showing the same address. Other businesses require a notarized letter, or a certificate from the city where domestic partnership status was obtained (unfortunately, this leaves people from many cities and most every small town out in the cold). Check with the individual company ahead of time, and if you don't like what you hear, try another company.

Travel-related businesses prove their commitment to the gay and lesbian market in other ways, too. Companies that treat their gay employees better, and who spend money researching and advertising to the gay market, are bound to be more sensitive to the needs of gay and lesbian travelers. And this sensitivity can translate into greater convenience—sometimes even savings—for you.

So how do you save money by renting cars from a gay-friendly company?

It comes down to that annoying "extra driver" charge. When I rent a car with friends, we usually designate one person as the driver, in order to avoid the charge.

When I rent with my boyfriend (excuse me, domestic partner), I don't have to worry about additional fees. That's because we rent only from companies that waive the extra driver fees for same-sex couples, just as they do for married heterosexuals.

In 1994, Avis became the first car rental company to waive these fees. Soon after, National Interrent did the same thing.

You still need to shop around, because several companies still charge the fees (some even charge married heteros—at least that penalizes both groups equally).

The documentation required to prove domestic partnership varies; sometimes all you need is identification showing the same address. Check with the car rental company ahead of time. And be sure to ask about that fee: it's nice to know you can actually save money while supporting companies that recognize the validity of our relationships.

7

CLASSIC GAY DESTINATIONS

> "Gay travelers have a resource other visitors
> don't: a built-in international community of
> "our own."
>
> —Lindsy Van Gelder and Pamela Robin Brandt,
> from the book *Are You Two . . . Together?*

I'd heard about the Meat Rack for a long time.

Nestled between Cherry Grove and the Pines—Fire Island's
two gay communities—it was a no-man's land of trees, bushes,
and sand. It was also the setting for countless stories of breath-
less, anonymous sexual encounters between some of the
hottest men in the New York area.

I had to see this for myself. Of course, that wasn't the only
reason I wanted to visit—after all, Fire Island is one of the top
gay destinations in the country. So now that I was here for the
first time, I just *had* to see whether the Meat Rack really
deserved its name.

After a few hours at the beach, my friend Rich and I had a
drink at the Ice Palace disco and waited for the sun to go down.

Then it was time to head over to the forbidden territory. We made our way to the end of the narrow boardwalk and soon found ourselves standing in the dark, in the middle of the legendary Meat Rack. The outline of tall sand dunes loomed on one side of us, and a dark forested area leered at us on the other. Hanging from one tree were little plastic bags filled with condoms. The moon was shining just enough to highlight four paths leading in different directions from where we were standing.

"OK," Rich said. "Let's split up now, and we'll meet in an hour back at the bar." He headed down one of the paths and was swallowed up by the forest.

The air was completely still. I looked around. Branches crackled as footsteps shuffled through the sand somewhere nearby. I squinted but couldn't see anything. The sounds got louder. These noises were probably coming from some hot guy looking to have some fun.

But then my overactive imagination kicked in.

Suddenly, I was Valerie Harper being stalked in some obscure TV movie. I might as well have been wearing a bandana and a wraparound skirt. In my mind, I now realized these strange sounds were coming from an axe murderer who was surely going to butcher me if I didn't get out of that horrid place as soon as humanly possible.

I let out a whimper.

I ran down one path and found myself in the middle of the forest. The condoms dangling nearby laughed at me.

I ran back and heard more noises.

Finally, I found the right path. I ran all the way back to the Ice Palace and waited there for an hour, until Rich came back, all smiles.

"So did you have fun?" he asked.

"Yeah, it was great."

The lesson? You have to pick your travel experiences carefully. Not every gay-popular attraction can please every traveler—especially if you have no control over your own imagination.

Luckily, there are plenty of places to choose from. Even before the term "homosexual" was coined, our people were building so-called "gay ghettos" where we could feel comfortable. And this phenomenon has happened in the United States in a big way. No matter where you go, you're never far from a town where we're a powerful force—sometimes even the majority of the population!

Even though these cities and towns are incredibly diverse, they share a few common elements that help to identify lesbian and gay culture. Gay and lesbian destinations usually boast a thriving artistic community, for example, a tribute to our creativity. They usually offer substantial nightlife, perhaps an indicator of our fun-loving personalities and our common lack of children. An above-average array of outdoor activities available in many gay-popular destinations are proof of our love of nature and sports—as well as our constant quest for a good tan.

Some of the most popular destinations are listed in this chapter. I'm not going to rehash listings and information that you can find in other guides; instead, we'll take a broad, general survey of the *types of vacations* you can expect in each place, to help you pick out those which best suit your personal taste. The resources will help you get further, up-to-date information about the destination.

You can easily travel to these destinations on your own, although package deals are available as well. Mainstream companies offer independent travel packages to several of the most popular gay destinations, such as New York City, San Francisco, Los Angeles, Palm Springs, and Key West, in addition to other favorites like New Orleans, San Juan, Hawaii, and destinations abroad.

It's probably no surprise to you that there are more big destinations for men than for women. And while women are certainly welcome at many predominantly male destinations, one female traveler notes that "there's not much reason for a lesbian to go to a place like South Beach, unless she hangs out with a lot of men."

Of course, there are plenty of other places that are popular with lesbian and gay travelers. Even though they don't appear in these listings, cities like Chicago, Montreal, and Fort Lauderdale are among the many destinations that can offer an unforgettable gay vacation.

In other words, don't think that the list of gay and lesbian favorites is static. A number of cities that already have a lot to offer are jockeying to become the next hot spot. The **Philadelphia Convention & Visitors Bureau,** for example, began promoting gay and lesbian tour packages in 1996, in conjunction with **Gray Line Tours.** And Atlanta, the site of the 1996 Olympics, was the first Olympic city to boast a Gay and Lesbian Visitors' Center, complete with gay tourism information and even a coffee bar.

So keep your eyes open and your itinerary flexible. And try not to think of your vacation in terms of a TV movie. (See Chapter Nine for details on the special events mentioned in this chapter.)

Resources

Gray Line Tours (Philadelphia), 215-568-6111, www.graylinetours.com

Men on Vacation, 800-959-4636, www.menonvacation.com

Philadelphia Convention & Visitors Bureau, 215-636-3300, www.pcvb.org

THINGS TO THINK ABOUT FIRST   Do you prefer the city or the country? Lots of men or lots of women, or a little of both? What kind of accommodations and activities do you want? Do you prefer traveling during peak season, when the place is really jumping, or during a quieter time? What time of year will you be traveling and do the destination's weather and activities for that time of year appeal to you? What kind of accommodations do you prefer—what level of luxury and what location is best for you?

For houses at resorts: Houses with a view of the ocean or bay are more expensive than houses inland. What can you afford and what do you need?

QUESTIONS TO ASK THE TRAVEL PROVIDER   What's included in the daily rate (e.g., meals, activities)? What is the atmosphere like at the hotel/guest house? (E.g., are people nude?) Are any special discounts available? Do rooms have private baths? How far is the property from the beach/town/nightlife?

8

Year-Round Favorites

San Francisco, California

I was shocked the first time I went to San Francisco. Not by some kinky sex club, not by some horrible act of violence, not by some spectacular sale. I was shocked by people's friendliness. When I entered a store, people actually smiled and said hello.

Maybe that's not a big deal for you, but after living in New York City for ten years, it's surprising to find a large, cosmopolitan city with a heart.

But that's one of San Francisco's selling points. The city offers the friendliness and manageability of a smaller town with the diversity and activities of a large metropolis. Plus it's a hub for gay and lesbian culture worldwide.

Annual events include the gay and lesbian pride festival and the San Francisco International Lesbian and Gay Film Festival, both in June. During September, two events are particularly popular with the leather contingent: the Folsom Street Fair, a leather-oriented street festival, and the Mr. Drummer contest.

THE KIND OF VACATION YOU CAN EXPECT HERE Urban, cultural, plenty of bars and clubs with diversity of ethnicities, men and women. More of a sense of gay culture and history here than in any other city. Fairly reasonable array of accommodations. Easy to navigate through the city without a car, thanks to decent mass transit and taxis. Like New York City, San Francisco can be used as a jumping-off point for side trips to gay havens, such as Russian River.

Accommodations

Castillo Inn 48 Henry St.; 800-865-5112 or 415-864-5111 (mostly men, 4 rooms, rates between $60–$80). Located in the historically gay Castro district, this small property features rooms with microwave ovens and refrigerators. Baths are private and shared.

Dolores Park Inn 3641 17 Street bet. Dolores and Church St.; 415-621-0482 (gay/straight, 4 rooms, single, $99–$245; double, $139–$259, including breakfast). A Victorian home, filled with antiques, located in the Mission district. Rooms feature TV and some have private baths. The property features a sun deck, with tennis courts nearby. (non-smoking)

House O'Chicks Guesthouse 2162 15th St.; 415-861-9849 (women only, 2 rooms, $50–$100). This small property gets the award for most creative name. Rooms feature TV and VCR, and provide access to the kitchen. Located two blocks from Castro Street.

Inn on Castro 321 Castro St.; 415-861-0321, innoncastro2. com (men and women, 8 rooms, single, $100–$165; double, $115–$185). This renovated home features comfortable accommodations. Rates include full breakfast and evening brandy.

Joie de Vivre Hotels 800-SF-TRIPS or 415-835-0300, www. sftrips.com. This company represents eleven gay-friendly boutique hotels throughout San Francisco, including the Abigail, located near the Civic Center; the Nob Hill Lambourne, in the Financial District; and several in the Union Square area: the Andrews, the Orchard, the Commodore, and the Hotel Rex. All are hip, popular places, they're in convenient locations for various activities, and they feature full amenities—bath, phone, TV, if not more.

24 Henry Street 24 Henry St.; 415-864-5686 (mostly gay; 5 rooms, $65–$85; 3 suites and 1 apt., $109). Full amenities are available at this reasonably priced property. Include complimentary continental breakfast buffet.

For More Information

Deaf Gay and Lesbian Center, 415-255-0700. An organization offering support and social activities for hearing-impaired lesbians and gay men.

Gay and Lesbian Helpline, 415-772-4357. General support, information, and referrals for the lesbian and gay community.

Women's Building, 415-431-1180. Support and activities for lesbians in the Bay Area. www.womansbuilding.org

Other Sources of Information

A Different Light Bookstore, 489 Castro St., 415-431-0891, a wonderfully well-stocked lesbian and gay bookstore

Bay Area Reporter, 415-861-5019, general-interest weekly gay paper

Folsom Street Fair, 415-861-3247; wwwfolsomstreetfair.com

Icon, 415-282-0942, monthly newspaper for lesbians

Mr. Drummer Contest, 415-252-1195

San Francisco Bay Times, 415-227-0800, general-interest biweekly gay paper; www.sfbaytimes.com

San Francisco International Lesbian and Gay Film Festival, 415-703-8650

West Hollywood, California

"When my gay male friends visit me here for the first time, they're kind of amazed," says Joseph, who moved to West Hollywood from the Midwest. "It's a little overwhelming, I guess."

West Hollywood is the trendy center of gay life for the gargantuan region known as greater Los Angeles. You'll hear plenty of jokes about vapidness and superficiality here, but the truth is that with a little good judgment, you can meet nice people here too. It may be a little distracting at first, though, wading through all the beauty.

Accommodations within the area are rather limited, with few reasonably priced standouts. **The San Vicente,** however, received an editor's choice award from *Out & About* and is conveniently located for most activities.

Annual events in the region include the lesbian and gay pride festival in June; Outfest, a gay and lesbian film and video festival in July; and Labor Day LA, which is four days of fund-raising parties in September.

THE KIND OF VACATION YOU CAN EXPECT HERE   West Hollywood is largely gay male, with plenty of gym bodies, beach bunnies, and star searchers. Emphasis is on nightlife, although showbiz-style sight-seeing is easy to arrange, and the ocean, mountains, and desert are all relatively close by. It's difficult to find accommodations right in the "middle of it all" in the gay section, and a car is crucial because, as that old song goes, "nobody walks in L.A." Laguna Beach is a popular gay beach about an hour away if the traffic is agreeable.

Accommodations

Rennaissance Beverly Hills Hotel   1224 S. Beverwil Dr., Beverly Hills; 310-277-2800 or 800-421-3212; www.renaissance hotel.com (gay/straight, 137 rooms, call for rates or check Website). Fully appointed rooms with balconies are the norm at this upscale establishment.

Hollywood Roosevelt   7000 Hollywood Blvd.; 800-950-7667 or 213-466-7000; www.hollywoodroosevelt.com (gay/straight, 321 rooms, $89–$249/$79–$209). Rooms have full amenities, access to large pool.

Holloway Motel   8465 Santa Monica Blvd.; 213-654-2454 (gay/straight, 22 rooms, $55–$65). Full amenities; some have kitchenettes. Walking distance to some gay bars.

Mondrian   8440 Sunset Blvd.; 800-525-8029 or 213-650-8999; www.mondrianhotel.com (gay/straight, 245 rooms, $310–$570). You'd better believe the rooms are fully appointed in this hotel, a favorite haunt of numerous celebrities.

Le Montrose   900 Hammond St., W. Hollywood, CA 90069; 800-776-0666 or 310-855-1115; www.lemontrose.com (gay/straight,

132 rooms, $195–$460). Room categories include standard, junior suite, executive suite, and one-bedroom suite. All are fully appointed, and some have kitchenettes, wet bar, modem line, fireplaces, balconies. Heated pool, hot tub, tennis court, exercise room. Le Montrose offers gay pride packages during the June festivities.

Ramada West Hollywood   8585 Santa Monica Blvd.; 310-652-6400 or 800-845-8585; www.ramada–wh.com (gay/straight, 175 renovated rooms, $109–$250). Suites with kitchenettes, multiline telephones with voice mail, fax, fireplace, private balconies, twice-daily maid service. On the property is a restaurant, rooftop pool and Jacuzzi, lighted free tennis court, on-site tennis pro, health club with private trainers, bicycles, and jogging.

San Vicente Inn & Resort   845 San Vicente Blvd.; 310-854-6915. Fax 310-289-5929; www.sanvicenteinn.com (gay, 30 rooms, $69–$259). A variety of price categories includes rooms with shared baths all the way up to suites and cottages. Solar-heated pool, hot tub, and clothing-optional sun deck.

For More Information

Gay and Lesbian Community Center of Long Beach, 562-434-4455, www.centerlb.org

Gay and Lesbian Community Center of Los Angeles, 323-993-7400 and 1-800-500-5287.

Gay and Lesbian Community Center of Orange County, 714-534-0961, www.thecenteroc.org

Sources for Additional Information

Edge Magazine, 213-962-6994. www.edgemagazin.com. Easy-to-read gay men's paper with plenty of party information.

Frontiers, 213-848-2222, www.frontiersweb.com. News and information about the region and the nation.

New York City

New York City is an overwhelming swirl of sights and sensations. For hyperactive gay and lesbian travelers, it's perfect.

Nonstop activity takes many forms: parties, bars, and clubs pump up the nightlife all week. Heavily gay neighborhoods abound, although the traditional gay hub, Greenwich Village, has been upstaged by Chelsea, the gymboy neighborhood just to the north. Gay and lesbian enclaves also thrive in Queens and Brooklyn, with Park Slope serving as home to many lesbians and Jackson Heights, Queens, the base for a large gay Latino community.

A wide array of cultural attractions can be found here: from the stars on Broadway to the Empire State Building, the Metropolitan Museum of Art to the Statue of Liberty.

The Big Apple is host to an array of annual events. In February, scads of gay men don white apparel for the Saint-at-Large White Party, a major event that recalls the days of the Saint, one of New York's premier gay discos. Held in a different location each year (the club itself no longer exists), it's a fund-raiser and an excuse to party at the same time. Colors are reversed the following month for the Saint-at-Large Black Party, which features more of the same, except with everyone wearing black. June witnesses one of the largest gay and lesbian pride celebrations in the country, with an entertaining rally one week before the massive parade, plus a street festival, and an overwhelming number of parties, events, and gatherings.

The party circuit continues in October, with the All Saint's Party and the Saint-at-Large Party, while New York's Halloween Parade is a huge, gay-and-straight event that jams the streets of Greenwich Village with people in costume. Many parties at gay and lesbian clubs follow the same evening. And in November, the big event is the AIDS Dance-a-thon, a benefit for the Gay Men's Health Crisis that offers the chance to wear out your feet for a good cause, while enjoying appearances by numerous celebrities.

If you're visiting from anywhere else in the United States, be prepared: New York can be expensive. It's also a tough, crowded city, and people may come across as unfriendly at times. Take it all in stride. The city has a lot to offer.

THE KIND OF VACATION YOU CAN EXPECT HERE   Lesbians and gay men come from all over the world to sample the mainstream cultural attractions as well as the gay and lesbian highlights.

Shopping, museums, and shows can fill up many days and evenings. Nightlife is vibrant, and bars and clubs for gay men are so numerous that they have become increasingly specialized in their clientele and atmosphere (for example, there are two which are mostly Asian, several are mostly for Latinos, a couple are for transvestites and their admirers, and several cater to particular fetishes). Subways and buses, in addition to those ubiquitous yellow taxis, are the best way to get around town; having your own car is almost a liability when looking for parking. Hotels are rather pricey, so if you have a friend you can stay with, do it. New York City is not much of an outdoorsy destination in itself (although the number of gay men roller-blading through Chelsea is ever growing), so you'll have to arrange for a side trip to Jones Beach or Fire Island if you want to catch some rays. Just make sure you go when the weather's warm—winters can be near-brutal, and summers sometimes are, too.

Accommodations

New York B&B Reservation Center   212-977-3512

Chelsea Pines Inn   317 W. 14th St., New York, NY 10014; 212-929-1023; www.chelseapinesinn.com (mostly men; 23 rooms, $89–$219). A town house with garden, located conveniently near the gay-popular neighborhoods of Chelsea and the Village. Some rooms have private baths; all have TV, phone, air-conditioning, refrigerators. Continental breakfast served on-site.

Colonial House Inn   318 W. 22nd St., New York, NY 10011; 800-689-3779 or 212-243-9669; www.colonialhouseinn.com (men and women; 20 rooms, $80–$160). Another town house, complete with sun deck on the roof, right off the ever-popular Eighth Avenue strip of gay businesses. Eight rooms have private baths.

Incentra Village House   32 Eighth Ave., New York, NY 10014; 212-206-0007 (gay/straight, 12 rooms; $119–$169). Yet another good location, in between the Village and Chelsea. Rooms feature TV, phone, air-conditioning; all have private bathrooms and some have working fireplaces.

For More Information

Gay and Lesbian Switchboard, 212-777-1800.

Homo Xtra, 212-352-3535 www.hx.com. A source for weekly party information.

Next, 212-627-0165. Similar to Homo Xtra, with plenty of party and club tips.

LGNY, 646-473-1985, www.lgny.com. News for lesbian and gay New Yorkers.

New York Blade, www.nyblade.com. Another popular gay newspaper.

9

SEASONAL FAVORITES

Fire Island, New York

"It's like one big brunch," says Rich Volo, a New Yorker who's spent alternating summer weekends on Fire Island for the past several years. "There's no other place that's like it in the world. It's a totally gay community, right on the beach, and they don't even allow cars. It's totally relaxing."

Relaxing, yes—easy to get to, not really. But maybe that helps preserve Fire Island's unique atmosphere. You've got to really *want* to come to this gay haven, if you are to endure the ninety-minute ride on the Long Island Railroad from New York City, followed by the taxi or van ride to the ferry boat that whisks you across the waters to this magical island. (Express bus service does go directly to the ferry terminal from Manhattan, but it still takes a while to get there.) During the warm months between Memorial Day and Labor Day, thousands of gay people a day make this trek.

Fire Island is a long, skinny island off the southern coast of Long Island. It comprises several predominantly vacation-oriented communities—the two gay ones are the Pines and Cherry Grove. Each has its own flavor: "Cherry Grove has more Long Islanders and lesbians and people who let their hair down," explains Rich. "The houses are cheaper and less glamorous. Cherry Grove, which was built before the Pines, has more luxurious houses and lots of Manhattanites—gay boys who work out at the gym."

Both communities are characterized by a lack of automobiles—instead, people pull little red wagons with supplies down the wooden boardwalks that crisscross the forested areas. Adding to this quaintness is the sizable population of deer that wander throughout the area, perfectly adjusted to the countless homosexuals that invade every year.

In between the two communities is the infamous "Meat Rack"—a region of sand dunes, gnarly trees, and bushes—which serves as a late-night, open-air sex club for some Fire Island inhabitants.

Summer festivities at both neighborhoods reach a fevered pitch during the GMHC Morning Party in August, which fills the beach with some five thousand people—mostly gay men, who party hard and raise funds for the Gay Men's Health Crisis.

Fire Island differs from most gay resorts in that it doesn't offer a wide variety of accommodations. Few people come for a one- or two-night visit: Most people rent houses for part of the summer (it's possible to find a share for a one-time visit, if you're lucky—otherwise check out the few inns in the neighborhood, but make reservations early).

Because of the cost and limited number of houses, finding a house—and the people to share it with—has become a complicated annual ritual for many gay men. "By the end of August, people are already thinking about next year's shares," says Rich. "All winter long, you can look for one. Go out and visit in January, or call a real estate broker. You've got to have eight, twelve or sixteen people total for the house. If you're only one or two people, you should go to the Sharathon."

The Sharathon is a gathering at New York City's Lesbian and Gay Community Services Center, held once a month during January, February, March, and April.

Hundreds of people come here, either to find additional roommates to fill their summer home, or to find a house that needs additional people to fill it up. So whether you already have a share set up on Fire Island or not, you're bound to find what you need. You'll also become an expert in the unique vocabulary of Fire Island (a "half-share," for example, is a space every other weekend; a "full share" is every week).

"It's hard to find a share with people that you like in a house you like," warns Rich. "Make sure you have a good idea of the kind of house you want, and the kind of people you can get along with."

THE KIND OF VACATION YOU CAN EXPECT HERE   Like many gay resorts, hedonism is pervasive. "There is some drug use and it's kind of a party environment," says Rich. There is limited, but extremely popular, nightlife in both the Pines and the Grove, and during special events both can be extremely crowded. The biggest annual event is the Morning Party, a fundraiser for the Gay Men's Health Crisis in August. Daylight hours are usually spent at the beach, or recuperating from partying the night before.

Accommodations

Prices listed are weekend/weekday prices, respectively. Most properties are closed during the colder months.

The Belvedere   P.O. Box 4026, Cherry Grove; 631-597-6448; www.thebelvedere.com (men only, 40 rooms, $300–$400/ $80–$100). A splashy combination of architectural styles mark this mansion. Amenities include a hot tub, gym, roof deck, and pool.

Carousel Guest House   185 Holly Walk, Cherry Grove; 631-597-6612 (gay/lesbian, 11 rooms, $65–$135, including breakfast). Property features sun deck, continental breakfast. Some rooms have private baths.

Cherry Grove Beach Hotel   Bayview Walk, Cherry Grove; 631-597-6600 (gay/lesbian, 57 rooms, $300–$400/$80–$120). This hotel, whose rooms have standard amenities, adjoins the Ice Palace Disco and features a large pool.

Dune Point   Lewis Walk, Cherry Grove; 631-597-6261 (gay/lesbian, 6 units, $75/$55); www.dunepoint.com Open year-round, Dune Point features a shared kitchen and baths, plus a TV room.

Holly House   Holly Walk, Cherry Grove; 631-597-6911 (gay/lesbian, 4 rooms, $90–$180, including breakfast). This property, which features basic amenities, is only open seasonally. Complimentary drink at your arrival.

Pines Place   P.O. Box 5309, Fire Island Pines; 631-597-6162 (7 rooms, $200–$275/$100–$175). This property features a sun deck, hot tub, and basic rooms, some with private bath.

Real Estate Agents

Bob Howard, 631-597-9400
Island Properties, 631-597-6360
Pines Harbor, 631-597-7575

Resources

There is no chamber of commerce or general information number for Fire Island, although individual properties, clubs, and real estate agents may be able to answer general questions.

Key West, Florida

The first time I visited Key West was as a teenager in the late 1970s, with my Uncle Ed and Aunt Agnes. As we walked down one of the many lovely streets in the historic district, we passed by a bar with doors wide open and disco music blaring. A few men were sitting at the bar inside, watching the sidewalk. My uncle glanced in, his eyes big and his mouth crooked. "I think that's a gay bar!" he said, astonished. I would have given anything to have been able to go in and verify that for him, but it would be many years before I could come back and actually do so.

Astonishment may be the reaction of some straight tourists who stumble unknowingly onto Key West's gay and lesbian culture, but it's not the attitude of the residents. The city of Key West has long recognized the contributions of its gay people, and they know how much we're worth as tourists, too.

The **Key West Business Guild,** the city's gay chamber of commerce, is an aggressive promoter of the city as a gay paradise throughout the year.

Like any gay destination worth its salt, Key West hosts several events and festivals. September's Womenfest Key West attracts thousands of women from across the country for a bunch of activities, including a wet T-shirt contest, a "Tea by the Sea," comedy nights, and even a tennis tournament. Events take place at a number of properties throughout Key West, and early reservations are recommended.

Also popular is the Key West Gay Arts Festival, which attracts a wide variety of artwork, along with artisans and their admirers, from across the country and abroad. Several days of exhibits and events offer visitors the chance to see the latest creations, as well as the chance to buy some of them.

In September, new theatrical works and old favorites get their deserved attention at the Key West Theatre Festival. Local and visiting writers and performers show off their stuff at various locations on the island, with specially priced tickets available to performances.

FantasyFest is one of the best-known festivals on the island, when thousands of people come out to celebrate Halloween with outrageous costumes and equally outrageous parties. The celebration actually lasts several days, and includes street fairs, a yacht race, food and arts celebrations, numerous costume competitions and fund-raisers, and, of course, the crowning of the King and Queen of FantasyFest. The excitement culminates in the FantasyFest parade, which is followed up with costume competitions and lots of parties. It's a Halloween that could only happen in Key West.

THE KIND OF VACATION YOU CAN EXPECT HERE   Key West is larger than gay resort towns like Provincetown and Fire Island. It's also straighter, although this is not necessarily a bad thing. One of the advantages is year-round good weather, and an impressive array of guest houses and hotels, including noteworthy properties like the Brass Key, which boasts pleasant accommodations, a heated pool, and a spa. Like most resort towns, there is more nightlife here for men than for women, but day and nighttime activities, both indoors and outdoors, offers a wide variety of entertainment. And the people are friendly!

Accommodations

Prices listed are in-season/off-season. In-season is generally from fall through Memorial Day; call for specific dates.

Alexander's   1118 Fleming St.; 305-294-9919 or 800-654-9919; www.alexanderskeywest.com (mostly gay and lesbian, 17 rooms, $145–$300/$80–$180). Numerous sun decks, heated pool, TV, and phones in room. The property offers continental breakfast, as well as cocktails on Friday and Saturday evenings. A favorite.

Ambrosia House   615 Fleming St.; 800-535-9838 or 305-296-9838; www.ambrosiakeywest.com (mostly gay, 6 carefully restored buildings, $158–$379/$110–$279). While this small guest house doesn't have a kitchen to offer full meals, the rooms feature refrigerators and coffee makers in each room.

Big Ruby's   409 Applerouth La.; 800-477-RUBY or 305-296-2323; www.bigrubykeywest.com (mostly gay, 17 rooms, $80–$350). Rooms at this guest house feature TV, refrigerator, air-conditioning. The property offers a full breakfast and hosts a weekly wine party.

Colours Key West   (Marrero's Guest Mansion); 410 Fleming St.; 800-ARRIVAL or 305-294-6977; www.colours.net (gay men, 12 rooms, $125–$210/$90–$170). This guest house, set in a nineteenth-century Victorian mansion, features a pool and what they call "special attention."

Coral Tree Inn   822 Fleming St.; 800-362-7477 or 305-296-2131; www.oasiskeywest.com (men only, 12 rooms, $169–$199/$105–$149). A nineteenth-century guest house that features complimentary breakfast, wine, and hors d'oeuvres. The property also features a pool and whirlpool, and rooms have private balconies.

Curry House   806 Fleming St.; 800-294-6777 or 305-294-5233; www.gaytraveling.com/curryhouse (men only, 9 rooms, $140–$190/$85–$120). Seven of the rooms at this nineteenth-century home have private baths, the remaining two share a bathroom. Curry House offers a full hot breakfast and a complimentary happy hour, plus pool and Jacuzzi. All rooms come equipped with air-conditioning, fans, refrigerators, and clock radios.

Cypress House   601 Caroline St.; 800-525-2488 or 305-294-6969 (men only, 16 rooms, $130–$250/$99–$180). One block away from Duval Street, Cypress House offers nude sunbathing and swimming. Continental breakfast served daily, as well as poolside cocktail hour with hors d'oeuvres. www.cypresshousekw.com

Florida Key Guesthouse   412 Frances St.; 800-932-9119 or 305-296-4719 (mostly gay and lesbian, 15 rooms, $140–$230/$65–$140). Plenty of sun decks, heated pool, and spa. Another *Out & About* award winner.

Island House for Men   1129 Fleming St.; 800-890-6284 or 305-294-6284; www.islandhousekeywest.com (men only, clothing optional, 34 rooms, $89–280). This frisky guest house features a Jacuzzi, sauna, gym, pool, and a room for TV and videos. A cafe on-site serves meals, and all rooms feature a lock box to protect those valuables.

La Terraza/La Te Da   1125 Duval; 877-528-3320 or 305-296-6706; www.lateda.com (mostly gay, $175–$225/$100–$150). A compound that includes two bars and a restaurant. The large pool, sun decks, and location make this a popular choice. Some rooms have private Jacuzzis.

Lighthouse Court Guesthouse   902 Whitehead; 305-294-9588; www.lighthousecourt.com (men only, 42 rooms, $95–$325/$60–$185). This property takes up over half an acre and features sun decks, heated pool, cafe, bar, Jacuzzi, and health club.

Lime House Inn   219 Elizabeth St.; 800-374-4242 or 305-296-2978 (men only, 11 rooms, $125–$200/$75–$130). Gardens, pool, and heated spa are the features of the Lime House Inn. Rooms feature kitchens, phones, TV, and air-conditioning. Breakfast is served daily, and happy hour lights up every afternoon. (e-mail: limehseinn.@aol.com)

Newton Street Station 1414 Newton St.; 800-248-2457 (men only, clothing optional, 7 rooms, $80–$150/$60–$100). Continental breakfast is served daily at this self-described "friendly, intimate" guest house, where rooms feature air-conditioning and TV, and guests enjoy a heated pool, gardens, and the free use of bicycles.

Oasis Guest House 823 Fleming; 305-296-2131 800-362-7477 (men only, 20 rooms, $169–$225/$109–$169). Complimentary breakfast is served at this restored 1895 mansion, as well as wine and hors d'oeuvres. Two pools, sun decks, and a Jacuzzi offer ample opportunity to enjoy the sunshine.

Rainbow Pearl's 525 United St.; 800-749-6696 or 305-292-1450; www.pearlsrainbow.com (women only, 39 rooms, $109–$249/$89–$199/$69–149). Women can enjoy themselves in Rainbow pool, 2 hot tubs, patio bar and grill and tropical gardens. Complimentary continental breakfast.

Resources

Key West Business Guild, 305-294-4603 or 800-535-7797, www.gaykeywestfl.com. The city's gay chamber of commerce.

Southern Exposure Guide, 305-294-6303, www.gaykeywest. net. Gay party columns and dish.

Miami Beach, Florida

From the moment you cross the causeway that links Miami Beach with the city of Miami, you'll know you're in a different world. Bizarre and beautiful art deco buildings line the streets, many of which are crowded with bizarre and beautiful people.

Miami Beach—in particular the southernmost art deco haven called South Beach—has taken its place as one of the "hippest" destinations for gay and straight people. After years of decay and neglect, gay people played a big role in restoring the art deco treasures and bringing in an ultrafashionable crowd. Indeed, South Beach has become a magnet for the fashion world, and it's not uncommon to see photo shoots taking place on the street in front of your hotel. And those high-cheekboned models share the sidewalks with elderly retirees, Cuban immigrants, and scantily clad gay boys with tight abs. It's an eclectic mix of people you won't find anywhere else.

One of the nicest surprises about South Beach is that it's not necessarily expensive to stay there. Sure, if you want an ocean-view room or a suite where Madonna once partied, you'll easily drop several hundred bucks a night. But there are still reasonably priced art deco hotels—such as the Kenmore, which even has a pool—along Washington and Collins Avenues, within three blocks from the beach and close to all the gay bars and shopping. Most of them are not gay establishments per se, but believe me, in a neighborhood like South Beach, they are quite accustomed to our type and are most hospitable. These are small hotels and don't follow the standard American pattern of uniformity. Some rooms may not have televisions, some may not even have phones. But you didn't come here to stay in your room anyway, did you?

Mark Porter, a visitor from Chicago, says that Miami is perfect for "people who like an urban edge in a tropical setting. There's also the high style, which coexists with some of the seedier aspects of urban living. It's the closest you'll come to New York without being in New York." With cheap airfares readily available, many gay men regularly make the few hours' trek from the Northeast.

Once they've arrived in South Beach, most gay people don't cross the causeway back to the mainland again until it's time to go home. But if you have a rental car and are up for some adventure, you can visit some of the campy tourist attractions in the Miami area—including Parrot Jungle, where our feathered friends dance, sing, and play musical instruments. Or take a driving tour of Calle Ocho, the closest thing to Havana in this country, Little Haiti, and Opa Locka, a mostly run-down town originally fashioned to conjure up the enchantment of the Arabian Knights (the city hall is a fanciful Arabian castle).

Of course, there's a whole state outside of Miami Beach just waiting to be discovered, as well. Companies like Miami Beach-based **Connections Tours** can tailor a gay vacation to fit your needs throughout Florida.

THE KIND OF VACATION YOU CAN EXPECT HERE   Activities in South Beach center around the beach and the bars. If you get bored, you can also rent rollerblades and mopeds to see more of the neighborhood and take in some more of that art deco charm. Trendy shops, mixed with a few fun tacky ones, offer additional diversion. Unfortunately, there is very little that is specifically targeted to lesbians.

Accommodations

Note: All the hotels listed here are gay-friendly and boast a substantial number of gay guests. Prices listed are peak/off-peak, respectively. Peak season is generally from fall through spring; call for specific dates.

Astor   956 Washington Ave.; 305-531-8081; www.hotelastor. com (41 rooms, $110–$900) (suite). Rooms at this property feature standard amenities plus a minibar and VCR. A small pool is also on-site.

Avalon   700 Ocean Dr.; 800-933-3306 or 305-538-0133; www. southbeachhotels.com (106 rooms, $89–$195). Like many South Beach properties, the rooms here flaunt art deco styling, in keeping with the overall architectural style. Rooms feature standard amenities plus safes; some also have refrigerators. An exercise room is available for guests. The restaurant, A Fish Called Avalon, is highly recommended.

Best Western South Beach   1020 Washington Ave.; 305-532-1930 (30 rooms, $135 and up). Full amenities are featured at this reasonably priced sister of the Kenmore, with which it shares a pool.

Casa Grande   834 Ocean Dr.; 800-688-7678 or 305-672-7003; www.thecasagrandehotel.com (an Island Outpost property, 32 rooms, $295–$525/$150 and up). **Island Outpost,** a hip young hotel company founded by former Island Records chief Chris Blackwell, runs a number of stylish, worthwhile places in South Beach, and this is one of them. Studios and one- and two-bedroom suites feature Southeast Asian fabrics, with full amenities and kitchens, VCRs, stereos and CD players, minibars, and safes. Some have terraces. www.islandoutpost.com

Cavalier 1320 Ocean Dr.; 800-688-7678 or 534-2135 (an Island Outpost property, 45 rooms, $175–$395/$130–$275). This property, conveniently close to the gay beach, features full amenities plus VCR, stereo and CD player, a safe, fresh flowers, and bottled water. Discounts are offered at a nearby gym. www.islandoutpost.com

Century 140 Ocean Dr.; 305-674-8855; www.centuryhotel soup.com (48 rooms, $125 and up/$75–$275). Rooms display artwork and feature full amenities and extras. Categories include standard, deluxe studio, and suite.

Colours at the Mantell Guest Inn, 255 W. 24th St.; 305-531-3601; www.colours.net (mostly gay, 24 studio apartments, $69–$99). Full amenities plus kitchenettes, safer sex supplies, in-room laundry facilities. The property features a pool and a gym.

Delano 1685 Collins Ave.; 305-672-2000; www.ianschrager hotels.com (208 rooms, $225–$375, suites $400–$700/$170–$250, suites $375–$700). Full amenities abound at this trendy place, which also features a gym and restaurant.

Essex 1001 Collins Ave.; 800-553-7739 or 305-534-2700; www. Essexhotel.com (59 rooms, $75–$125). Full amenities and a good location.

Impala 1228 Collins Ave.; 305-673-2021; www.hotelimpala miamibeach.com (17 rooms, $189–369/$159–$315). The Impala's standard, deluxe room features full amenities with a queen-sized bed, TV/VCR/CD player, voice mail, bottled water, complimentary continental breakfast, and use of CD and video libraries. The one-bedroom suites offer the same amenities, plus a wet bar, refrigerator, and two separate phone lines. The grand suite tops off all these amenities with vaulted ceilings, a reading area, and a balcony.

Jefferson House   1018 Jefferson Ave.; 305-534-5247 (7 rooms, $99–$159, 1 suite, $205/$155). Full amenities plus a pool.

Kenmore   1050 Washington Ave.; 305-674-1930; www.pwr sort.com (50 rooms, $125–$195/$79–$83). This reasonably priced property features full amenities, plus in-room refrigerators and a pool shared with the Park Washington. Conveniently located across the street from a gay bar called Twist.

Kent   1131 Collins Ave.; 800-688-7678; www.islandoutpost. com (an Island Outpost property, 54 rooms, $145–$250/ $130–$250). Each room features full amenities plus TV, VCR, CD stereo system, two phone lines with voice mail, minibar, safe, and access to Club Body Tech Gym.

Lily Guest House   835 Collins Ave.; 305-535-9900; www.lily guesthouse.com (17 rooms, $130–$150/$110–$140). Studios and suites with full amenities; property features sun deck and patio.

Marlin   1200 Collins Ave.; 800-538-9076 or 305-673-8770; www.islandoutpost.com (an Island Outpost property, 12 rooms, year-round rates, $195–$415). Dramatic art deco confection that's a favorite of recording stars and other celebrities. The all-suite property features TV, VCR, CD stereo system, two-line phone system with voice mail, fresh flowers in every room, batik robes, iron, hair dryer, in-room safes, and access to the Club Body Tech Gym nearby. A sun deck on the roof allows for views to the beach, one block away. Should you feel drawn to singing, a full-service recording studio is on the premises.

Park Central   640 Ocean Dr.; 800-727-5236 or 305-538-1611 (120 rooms, $175–$375/$125–$295). Full amenities plus clock radios, safes, refrigerators, bottled water, and, for some rooms, views of the ocean. The property also features a pool, restaurant/bar, and small gym. www.theparkcentral.com

Penguin   1418 Ocean Dr.; 305-534-9334; www.thepenguin hotel.com (44 rooms, $115–$145). This oceanfront hotel features full amenities, plus a restaurant and bar.

Raleigh   1775 Collins Ave.; 800-848-1775 or 305-534-6300; www.raleighhotel.com (107 rooms, $179–$279, suite, $607–$749/ call for off-season rates). The Raleigh, which was once a glamorous 1940s hotel, has come into its own once again, and boasts its own section of beach. The Blue Star is the hotel's award-winning restaurant. The stunning pool, which has its own bar, provides a popular photo opportunity. Rooms feature full amenities plus VCR, multiple telephones, a desk, queen-sized bed, and CD stereo system.

Florida Hotel Network   800-538-3616 or 305-538-2616. This company provides a gay reservation service for hotels and rental properties.

Resources

Greater Miami Convention & Visitors Bureau, 888-76-MIAMI, www.tropicoolmiami.com. General tourist information.

Lesbian, Gay, and Bisexual Community of Miami Beach, 305-531-3666. Services and information specific to Miami Beach.

South Beach Business Guild, 305-534-3336. Miami Beach's very own gay business guild can provide information about local gay and gay-friendly businesses.

Miami Beach Chamber of Commerce, 305-672-1270, www.miamibeachchamber.com. General tourism and business information about Miami Beach.

For More Information

Connections Tours, 800-OUT-TIME or 305-673-3153 (packaged trips to Florida destinations) www.connectionstours.com

Good Time Tours, 800-446-0886 or 850-476-0046 (packaged trips to Florida; official tour operator for Gay Day at Disney)

Hotspots, 954-772-0001. Florida's party paper. www.hotspots magazine.com

South Florida Fun, www.southfloridafun.com. Gay and lesbian listings for Miami, Miami Beach, Fort Lauderdale, Key West, and West Palm Beach.

Miami.com/Gay, South Florida news and information for visitors and locals.

The Weekly News, 305-757-6333, www.twnmag.com. Gay and lesbian news and information for greater Miami

Palm Springs, California

"Palm Springs is great because it's a warm-weather destination but it doesn't have the cheesy environment you sometimes get with beaches," says Marc Boisclair, a regular visitor to this popular California destination. "It's not run-down, it's safe, it's clean. And there's a lot of cute guys, too."

Imagine all the beauty of the California desert, all the fun of a gay-friendly destination—all situated just a couple hours east of Los Angeles. The range of accommodations for gay male travelers is impressive, ranging from quiet bed and breakfasts to gay hotels with an intensely sexual atmosphere. The expanded **InnExile** won one of *Out & About*'s Editor's Choice awards in the guest house category. There are a few properties that offer quality accommodations for lesbians, including **Delilah's Enclave,** also the recipient of an *Out & About* award.

Activities include sampling cuisine at gay restaurants, buying gifts for your friends at some of the many small shops, and spending the evenings in popular bars and discos.

Palm Springs heats up even more during special events. In March, the Dinah Shore Classic brings thousands of female golfers and fans—many of them lesbians—to the area. As a result, this championship exhibition of the world's best female golfers is also one of the largest lesbian gatherings in the world. In addition to several days of golf-intensive activities, parties and events especially for lesbians provide plenty of diversion, and the women-only guest houses fill up months in advance.

For gay men, the big event is the White Party, held on Easter weekend. Multiple parties and special entertainment from across the nation are highlights of the weekend, which raises funds for AIDS organizations. Again, since this is a major event for circuit party enthusiasts, the guest houses fill up fast, so make your plans early.

The region has plenty to offer beyond gay life and parties. The unique beauty of the desert in bloom, as well as soaring mountain ranges, beckon many visitors. There are several ways to enjoy this area's beauty. To get an overhead view, try a lofty cruise in a hot-air balloon, which features a pilot and guide, as well as complimentary champagne and the chance to see the backyards of some rich people's homes.

The Palm Springs Aerial Tramway offers dazzling views during its fourteen-minute ride up the side of Mt. San Jacinto— it also connects with the thirteen-thousand-acre Mount San Jacinto Wilderness State Park, which boasts fifty-four miles of hiking trails, five campgrounds, and a ranger station. The park's Nordic Ski Center is open from November 15 to April 15.

Another recommended activity is the Desert Adventures Jeep tour, which offers a variety of scenic excursions to the ancient Indian Canyons, the soaring cliffs of the Santa Rosa Mountains, and the Coachella Valley, accompanied by a naturalist guide. You can even pay a visit to the infamous San Andreas fault and see the dramatic setting where *Star Trek: The Motion Picture* was filmed.

Spring is the most popular season for Palm Springs. "I wouldn't recommend going there year-round," says Marc. "It can get really hot. You can't go there June, July, or August." Unless you're a real heat seeker, that is.

Accommodations

Some properties in Palm Springs list prices for three different seasons. The peak season is generally during the spring; off-peak is the summer; and from the fall through the beginning of winter is "shoulder season," when the weather is not quite as ideal as peak season, but it's much better than off-peak. Check with individual properties for details.

Alexander Barely Inn   598 Grenfall Rd.; 760-327-6911 or 800-448-6197, www.barelyinn.com (men only, 8 rooms, $95–$125). This guest house features full amenities plus VCR, in-room laundry facilities, safer sex supplies. Some rooms have a private patio and kitchen. Continental breakfast and a light lunch is served, and guests can go nude if they want at the pool and sun deck.

All World Resort   526 Warm Sands Dr.; 760-323-7505; www. allworldsresort.com (men only, clothing optional, 39 rooms, $79–$150). Full amenities plus VCRs, microwave ovens, and complimentary poolside continental breakfast. Two pools, two Jacuzzis, and hot tub with waterfall.

Alpine Gardens Hotel   1586 E. Palm Canyon Dr.; 619-323-2231; www.Alpinegardens.com (gay/straight, 11 rooms, $60–$115). Some of the rooms at Smoke Tree Villa have a kitchenette; all have full amenities. There's a pool and hot tub on the premises, and continental breakfast is served.

A Place in the Sun   754 San Lorenzo Rd.; 760-325-0254 or 800-779-2254; www.palmsprings.com (gay/straight, 17 units, $89–$210). Rooms feature full amenities, plus kitchenettes and private garden patios or courtyards. Heated pool and spa, laundry room, putting green, and access to tennis facilities. www.mirage4men.com

Bee Charmer   1600 E. Palm Canyon Dr.; 760-778-5883, 888-321-5699; www.beecharmer.com (women only, 13 rooms, $115–$145). This pleasant hotel for women features full amenities plus VCR, refrigerator, and microwave, as well as a pool.

Camp Palm Springs   722 San Lorenzo Rd.; 760-322-CAMP or 800-793-0063; www.camp-palm-springs.com (men only, clothing optional, 24 rooms plus 3-bedroom town house, summer, $69–$150/shoulder $79–$175/$99–$200). This property features a pool, spa, and tennis court. Complimentary breakfast and light lunch is offered daily, as well as evening cocktails. Rooms feature TV, VCR, and kitchenettes.

Canyon Club Hotel   960 N. Palm Canyon Dr.; 800-295-2582 or 760-322-4367; www.canyonclub.com (men only, clothing optional, 32 rooms, $79–$129). Rooms, which were recently renovated, have either one or two beds. All are air-conditioned, and include remote-control TV, cable, telephone, and refrigerator. Some rooms have full kitchens and some have private patios. In-house, all-male video channels available twenty-four hours a day. The property also features a fifty-foot pool, courtyard, sauna, and steam room.

The Columns   537 Grenfall Rd.; 760-325-0655 or 800-798-0655; www.pscolumns.com (men only, 7 rooms, $89–$109, $69–$89). Full amenities plus VCR, complimentary continental breakfast. The property features a pool and clothing-optional sunbathing.

Chestnutz Resorts   641 San Lorenzo Rd.; 760-325-5269 or 800-621-6973; www.chestnutz.com (men only, 12 rooms, $109–$268). This property features full amenities plus VCR; some rooms have kitchenettes. The property features a restaurant, pool, and Jacuzzi. Women only last week in March.

Desert Palms Inn   67–580 E. Palm Canyon Dr., Cathedral City; 760-324-3000 or 800-801-8696 (gay/lesbian, 29 rooms, $69–$109/ $49–$89). Rooms at this property offer full amenities. A mostly gay restaurant and bar are on-site, as well as a pool and hot tub.

Desert Paradise   615 Warm Sands Dr.; 760-320-5650 or 800-342-7635; www.desertparadise.com (men only, 14 rooms, $99–$250). Some of the rooms at this property have kitchenettes; all have full amenities as well as access to the hotel's pool and Jacuzzi.

El Alameda   175 El Alameda; 760-323-3977 or 888-547-7881 (men only, 15 rooms, $135–$235). Another Harlow Hotel property, El Alameda features full amenities plus VCR, modem line, and refrigerators. Continental breakfast and complimentary lunch are included, and the property also features a gym, pool, and sun deck, where nudity is allowed. www.harlowhotel.com

El Mirasol Villas   525 Warm Sands Dr.; 760-327-5913 or 800-327-2985; www.elmirasol.com (men only, 14 rooms, $100–$175). All the rooms at this property have kitchenettes, full amenities. Two pools are on-site.

Five-Fifty   550 Warm Sands Dr.; 760-320-7144 or 800-669-0550 (men only, clothing optional, 8 rooms, $79–$124). This hotel offers suites and studios with full amenities, plus kitchenettes and refrigerators. Nudity is acceptable at the pool and hot tub; continental breakfast is offered on-site.

Hacienda en Sueño   586 Warm Sands Dr.; 760-327-8111 or 800-359-2007; www.thehacienda.com (men only, 7 apts., $109–$229). Rooms here feature full amenities plus patios, VCR, in-room laundry facilities, kitchenettes with refrigerator and microwave.

Nudity is allowed at the two pools and hot tub. A library of books and videos is available to guests, and guest pantries provide sustenance on an honor system.

InnExile 545 Warm Sands Dr.; 760-327-6413 or 800-962-0186; www.innexile.com (men only, 31 rooms, clothing optional, $87–$116). Full amenities plus VCRs, complimentary breakfast, luncheon, and happy hour. 3 pools, Jacuzzi, gym, sauna, billiard room, and fireplace all on premises.

Mirage 555 Grenfall Rd.; 760-322-2404 or 800-669-1069; www.mirage4men.com (men only, 4 rooms, connected to Atrium and Vista Grande, clothing optional, $79–$195). Rooms at Mirage feature full amenities plus VCR, kitchenettes, and refrigerators. Nudity is allowed everywhere on the property, not just at the pool, sun deck, and gym.

Sago Palms 595 Thornhill Rd.; 760-323-0224 or 800-626-7246; www.sagopalmsresort.com (men only, clothing optional, 6 rooms, rates $79–$149). Room categories range from "bachelor" (studio) to one-bedroom suites, and feature the standard stuff plus VCR, in-room laundry facilities, kitchenettes. The suites have fireplaces. On-site features include pool, gym, and a hot tub; Sago Palms serves a continental breakfast to its guests.

Triangle Inn 555 San Lorenzo Rd.; 760-322-7993 or 800-732-7555, www.triangle-inn.com (men only, 9 rooms and suites, $99–$179/call for off-season rates). Full amenities plus stereos, kitchenettes, pool.

The Villa 67-670 Carey Rd., Cathedral City; 760-328-7211 or 800-845-5265; www.thevilla.com (mostly men, 44 rooms, $50–$125). This large property offers a relaxed atmosphere and full amenities plus wet bars and kitchenettes. A pool, hot tub, and sauna round out the hotel's offerings, while a mostly gay bar and restaurant feeds guests and visitors alike.

Vista Grande 574 Warm Sands Dr.; 760-322-2404 or 800-669-1069 (men only, 8 rooms, connected to Mirage, Atrium, and Avalon; clothing optional, $99–$195). Kitchenettes are among the amenities beyond the standard one and that are provided here, as well as VCRs. On the premises is a pool, hot tub, gym, and video library. Nudity is accepted at the pool and hot tub.

Vista Grande Resort Atrium   574 Warm Sands Dr.; 760-322-2404 or 800-669-1069 (men only, 40 rooms, clothing optional, connected to Mirage and Vista Grande, $79–$195). This resort property features full amenities plus kitchen, VCR (with access to X-rated videos), and safer sex supplies. Nudity is allowed at the pool and sun deck.

For More Information

The Bottom Line, 760-323-0552. News and information twice a month
Desert Community Directory. Listings of local gay and lesbian businesses
Palm Springs Gay Tourism Council, P.O. Box 2885, Palm Springs, CA 92263
Star Magazine, www.starmagazine.com. Offers information and entertainment options for the region

Provincetown, Massachusetts

"We've been coming here for years, and it never fails to surprise us how well people get along here," says Julie Thompson, who first visited Provincetown as a single woman and now vacations with her lover, Barb. "Plus, where else can you actually be in the majority as a homosexual?"

Not many other places. Every year, Provincetown (or P-town, as people so readily call it) continues to draw thousands of gay and lesbian visitors. Yes, this is one resort community with plenty of lesbians *and* gay men—and even the straight people seem to blend in nicely.

The Pilgrims landed in Provincetown—at the tip of what would one day be known as Cape Cod, Massachusetts—in 1620 and stayed about a month before moving on to Plymouth. Today, gay and lesbian vacationers land for the few months between Memorial Day and Labor Day—and an increasing number of people are enjoying the resort the whole year round. Crisp Victorian architecture graces the tiny streets of this picturesque community, while the sea air refreshes the weary urbanite.

"I love Provincetown's beauty," says Mark Porter, a snappy-dressing gay wit who flies to Cape Cod all the way from his home in Chicago. "I love the fact that it's kind of European. It's the best of all kinds of worlds. There are tea dances and discos and all the club life you'd want. And you get that urban sort of feel on the main Commercial Street, where there's a lot of people and a lot of shopping. But you can get on your bike and five minutes away you'll find nature—it's beautiful."

"I also like that there's a mix of gay men and lesbians," Mark adds. "The great thing about it is we're really in the majority. Most everything is geared toward our taste level."

Mark has stayed in private condos during his visits, which he arranges through In-Town Reservations (parent company **RSVP-town**), a company that arranges condo rentals and guest house stays. "That way," Mark explains, "you get a kitchen, and you save money—besides, the food's not that great here."

Most visitors stay at one of the seemingly limitless number of guest houses that dot Commercial Street and the side streets. Among the best is Six Webster Place, which was chosen by *Out & About* for an editor's choice award.

THE KIND OF VACATION YOU CAN EXPECT HERE   The fun centers around the beach during daylight hours, and the bars and clubs at night. Activities are on a lesser (but more diverse) scale than Palm Springs and Miami Beach, but much more lively than Saugatuck or Ogunquit. "Provincetown is extremely hedonistic," Mark claims. "For gay men, it's all about beautiful bodies, and that can get a little overwhelming." Natural beauty includes the dunes and beaches of the Cape Cod National Seashore, while whale watch cruises and bicycling provide additional diversions. Quiet times spent in the guest houses, or with friends, can provide a respite from the heavy partying.

Accommodations

Prices listed are in-season/off-season. In-season is generally the summer months and off-season is winter; some properties have additional rate schedules for other times of year.

Admiral's Landing   158 Bradford St.; 508-487-9665; www. admiralslanding.com (gay/lesbian, 6 rooms, 2 studio efficiencies, $115–$135/$50–$85). Some of the rooms in this guest house, set in an 1840s home, share bathrooms. Amenities include a continental breakfast and a shared TV lounge.

Anchor Inn   175 Commercial St.; 508-487-0432; www.anchor innbeachhouse.com (gay/lesbian, 25 rooms, $175–$375/ $105–$195). Rooms at this guest house feature TV and decks; some have air-conditioning, some have private baths. Continental breakfast is offered.

The Beaconlite   12 Winthrop St.; 508-487-9603; www.cape code.net/beaconlite (gay/lesbian, 16 rooms, call for rates). Rooms feature queen and double beds, TV, and refrigerator. Guests can take in the sun on the sun deck, and continental breakfast is offered.

The Boatslip   161 Commercial St.; 508-487-1669 (gay/ straight, 45 rooms, call for rates). This relatively large property offers rooms with TV and balconies; also on-site is a full-service restaurant, a pool, and sun deck, as well as a popular gay and lesbian bar.

The Brass Key Guest House   67 Bradford St.; 508-487-9005 or 800-842-9858; www.brasskey.com/ptown.htm (mostly gay/ lesbian, 12 rooms, $230–$425/$95–$240). An attractive, restored sea captain's home and two cottages surround a private courtyard with heated plunge pool. Full amenities plus VCR, refrigerators, fireplaces.

The Carriage House   7 Central St.; 508-487-3387, 800-309-0248; www.thecarriagehouse.com (gay/lesbian, 10 rooms, call for rates). Activity often centers around the hospitality room here, where the VCR and TV are. Available with rooms are private bath and TV.

Chicago House   6 Winslow St.; 508-487-0537, 800-733-7869 (gay/lesbian, 10 rooms, 3 apts., $55–$115/$35–$70).

Coat of Arms   7 Johnson St.; 508-487-0816 (men only, 11 rooms, call for rates). This Victorian guest house offers continental breakfast, and a common area with bar, piano, and stereo.

The Crown and Anchor   247 Commercial St.; 508-487-1430 (gay/straight, 28 rooms, $70–$115/$40–$85). Perfect for partying because it's literally on top of several nightspots, this property features basic amenities.

Crown Point   82 Bradford St.; 508-487-2213; www.crown point.com (40 rooms, 1 apt., $155–$360/$105–$280). Some rooms at this property have kitchenettes and air-conditioning. Continental breakfast is offered.

The Dunes Provincetown   125 Bradford St. Extension; 508-487-1956, 800-475-1833; www.thedunesprovincetown.com (13 rooms and 6 apts., call for rates). Full amenities characterize the motel rooms and apartment suites here, which also feature VCR and kitchenette.

Elephant Walk Inn   156 Bradford St.; 508-487-2543 or 800-889-9255; www.elephantwalkinn.com (gay/lesbian, 8 rooms, rates are between $56–$125). This property pretty successfully maintains the feeling of an Edwardian country house. Rooms feature air-conditioning, refrigerators, and ceiling fans, and a sun deck allows for the enjoyment of the rays.

Fairbanks Inn   90 Bradford St.; 508-487-0386, 800-324-7265; www.fairbanksinn.com (gay/straight, 16 rooms, call for rates). Some of the rooms in this guest house have private baths and kitchenettes.

Gabriel's   104 Bradford St.; 508-487-3232, 800-969-2643; www.gabriels.com (women and their friends, 20 rooms and apartments, $100–$200/$75–$110). Rooms at this attractive inn feature full amenities, plus VCR, air-conditioning, modem line, and kitchen. The property also features a hot tub, sauna, steam room, gym, and fax services, in addition to a full breakfast.

Gifford House   11 Carver St., 800-434-0130, 508-487-0688; www.giffordhouse.com (mostly men, 25 rooms, $90–$182/$50–$100). With a gay bar right on-site, it's a good place for guys looking to party. Rooms are basic, but if you're planning on going out a lot, they may be more than sufficient. Continental breakfast is offered.

Heritage House   7 Center St.; 508-487-3692 (gay/lesbian, 13 rooms, rates between $70–$110). This guest house, built in 1856, offers guest rooms with TV, VCR, and refrigerator. Continental breakfast is served on-site.

Lands End Inn   22 Commercial St.; 508-487-0706 (gay/straight, 17 rooms, call for rates). Some rooms at this property have private baths, some don't; none have phones. An interesting collection of antiques and curios make this property stand out.

Normandy House   184 Bradford St.; 508-487-1197 (gay/lesbian, 8 rooms, call for rates). Ocean views are a big draw at this guest house. Full amenities are available, plus VCR, kitchenettes, and refrigerators. Normandy House serves continental breakfast daily, and features a hot tub and sun deck.

Prince Albert Guest House   166 Commercial St.; 508-487-0859, 800-992-0859 (gay/lesbian, 7 rooms, 1 studio apartment, $90–$180/$65–$105). This guest house features air-conditioned rooms; the studio apartment also has a kitchen. Continental breakfast is served, and the house has a sun deck.

Ravenwood   462 Commercial St.; 508-487-3203; www.provincetown.com/ravenwood/index.html (mostly women, 1 room, 4 apts., call for rates). Rooms at this Greek Revival home offer full amenities, and some rooms and apartments offer full kitchens, ocean views, and private decks. A common sun deck is available for guests whose rooms lack their own, as well as a hot tub. (Non smoking)

Revere Guest House   14 Court St.; 508-487-2292, 800-487-2292 (gay/straight, 8 rooms, call for rates). This restored home, built sometime around 1830, features limited amenities in a comfortable, historic setting.

Seasons   160 Bradford St.; 508-487-2283, 800-563-0113; www.provincetownseasons.com (gay/lesbian, 5 rooms, $135/$80). Rooms here feature ceiling fans, private baths, and plenty of Victorian touches. Full breakfast is served. All room include color TV, VCR, and radio CD player. All rooms have AC in the summer.

Shire Max   5 Tremont St.; 508-487-1233; www.ptownlib.com/shiremax.html (7 rooms, 2 apts., call for rates). This bed and breakfast offers rooms with kitchenettes, TV and VCR, and bathrooms with hair dryers. A large video library is available to guests, as well as a tea time informal buffet, and sun deck.

Six Webster Place   6 Webster Place; 508-487-2266 (gay/lesbian, 6 rooms and 3 apts. Call for rates). A year-round historic home with five guest rooms, a luxury suite and three luxury apartments. Most have fireplaces, private baths, and cable TV. Outside are sun decks, a patio, and a nine-person Jacuzzi.

Somerset House   378 Commercial St.; 508-487-0383, 800-487-0383; www.somersethouseinn.com (gay/lesbian, 13 rooms, 1 apt., $110–$230/$90–$200/$75–$180). A well-restored nineteenth-century home with limited amenities, but elegant surroundings.

Swanberry Inn   8 Johnson St.; 508-487-4242 (mostly men, 10 rooms, call for rates). Attractive, comfortable rooms with shared baths mark this pleasant guest house.

Watership Inn   7 Winthrop St.; 508-487-0094, 800-330-9413; www.watershipinn.com (gay/lesbian, 17 rooms, $90–$145/$44–$65). Continental breakfast is included in the price at this guest house, where rooms feature TV, and some have private baths. A sun deck is available for all guests.

West End Inn   44 Commercial St.; 508-487-9555, 800-559-1220 (gay/lesbian, 5 rooms and 2 apts., rates $119–$229, $69–$129). This bed and breakfast features rooms with private and shared baths, TV, and VCR. The apartments also have a full kitchen. Outside the attractive white Greek Revival home, a sun deck invites guests to get some color.

Westwinds   28 Commercial St.; 508-487-1841 (gay/lesbian, 2 cottages, 2 apartments, call for rates). Full amenities mark the attractive apartments and cottages, which also include kitchens. A pool and deck are also on-site.

White Wind Inn   174 Commercial St.; 508-487-1526; 888-449-WIND; www.whitewindinn.com (gay/straight, 11 rooms, $115–$225/$75–$145). The former home of a nineteenth-century sea captain, this inn features full amenities plus VCR and refrigerator. Continental breakfast is served daily.

Resources

Cape Cod National Seashore, 508-349-3785

Provincetown AIDS Support Group, 508-487-9445, www.pasg online.org/

Provincetown Business Guild, 508-487-2313 or 800-637-8696, www.ptown.org. Gay and lesbian business and tourism information

Provincetown Chamber of Commerce, 508-487-3424

Provincetown Reservations System, 800-648-0364 (information and reservations for bed and breakfast properties)

RSVP-town, 4 Standish St., P.O. Box 1983, Provincetown MA 02657-0246. 800-67P-TOWN or 508-487-1883; www.province town.com/rsvptown. RSVP-town is a group of services: In-Town Reservations, Travel Network, and Provincetown Properties. These businesses can make travel arrangements and reservations for visitors to Provincetown. Their services are free of charge and include locating and making reservations at the more than one hundred twenty-five guest houses, inns, and motels they represent. They can also arrange airfare, car rental, and the rental of condos, houses, cottages, and apartments in the Provincetown area.

Saugatuck, Michigan

The Saugatuck area is a gay haven during the summer months. The region, which includes the town of Douglas, is a getaway for gay men and lesbians from Chicago, Detroit, Indianapolis, Toledo, and everywhere in between, serving much the same function for homosexual midwesterners as Provincetown does for their counterparts in the Northeast.

"Saugatuck has a lot going for it," says Mark Porter, a Chicago resident who has a country home just south of Saugatuck. "Physically, the area is beautiful, and the people are very respectful of gay visitors. The nightlife is more limited than a place like Provincetown, but it's still a great place to vacation."

In fact, most of the gay nightlife centers on The Dunes, a resort complex that features cabins, a hotel, multiple bars, and a disco. "It's not the trendiest place to go out, but it gets crowded and it's fun," says Mark. Sometimes, gay-popular bonfires at nearby locations pick up the slack as makeshift after-hours clubs.

The most popular daytime activities take place on or near the shore of Lake Michigan, where sunbathers (gay and straight) pack the beach and motorboats cruise the waters. A variety of shopping, antiques, and food is available in quaint Saugatuck.

"And don't forget about Holland," adds Mark, referring to a third popular town in the region. "It's a cool, kitschy day trip," he says. "You can visit the Dutch village and buy all kinds of wooden shoes there."

THE KIND OF VACATION YOU CAN EXPECT HERE   Gay men come here from throughout the region to relax, sun themselves, and party in equal measures. The nightlife is limited, but the place is packed wall-to-wall during the summer months. Daytime activities include sunning on the beach, swimming, boating, and antiquing.

Accommodations

Campit Campground   6635 118th Ave.; Fennville, MI; 616-543-4335 or 877-CAMPIT-1; www.saugatuckweekends.com (gay and lesbian, adults only, call for rates). Twenty-five wooded and open acres, with electrical hookups for RVs, tent campsites, and "Sturdy Girls Bunk 'n' Breakfast," a male/female bed and breakfast that offers continental breakfast and use of the campground facilities.

The Dunes Resort   333 North Blue Star Hwy; Douglas, MI 49406; 616-857-1401; www.dunesresort.com (mostly men, 72 rooms, 13 cottages, call for rates). *The* resort for gay men in the Saugatuck area. Fourteen acres filled with guest rooms, cottages, bars, a pool (also with bar), a disco, gift shop, and a full-service restaurant. Most rooms have full amenities.

Douglas House B&B   41 Spring St, Douglas, MI 49406-0801; 616-857-1119 (gay/straight, 4 suites call for rates). Formerly known as the Alpen Haus, this bed and breakfast is now under new ownership. It's located in the center of Douglas, convenient to the region's attractions, and features full amenities.

The Kirby House B&B   294 W. Center, Douglas, MI 49406; 800-521-6473, 616-857-2904, www.bbonline.com/milkirby (gay-friendly, 8 rooms, $85–$155). A pool, hot tub, and sun deck distinguish this guest house. Rooms feature full amenities plus VCR, kitchenettes, and fireplaces.

Resources

Saugatuck Area Business Association, 616-857-3133, www.saugatuckdouglas.com. General information about member businesses in the Saugatuck area.

Saugatuck-Douglas Convention & Visitors Bureau, 616-857-1701, www.saugatuck.com. This mainstream organization publishes a Saugatuck-Douglas visitors' guide with information about local businesses, activities, and attractions.

Ogunquit, Maine

"This place is kind of like the quieter sister of Provincetown," says Jeff Rickles, a seasonal regular at this resort town on the coast of Maine. "You get three miles of beach, some nice guest houses, and a gay community—but it's a lot more subdued."

That's one reason why lesbian and gay travelers show up here every summer: to take in the sun and enjoy the scenery, without the loud distractions that characterize larger gay-popular destinations. The town is not as intensely queer as Provincetown, either, but most people feel perfectly comfortable mingling with the straight tourists.

The selection of accommodations is rather limited, which may be one reason why hotels and guest houses fill up early here. Make plans as far ahead as you can.

THE KIND OF VACATION YOU CAN EXPECT HERE   Daytime activities include sunbathing and swimming at the gay section of the beach. In addition, sight-seeing is easy and enjoyable, with Kennebunkport, Wells, and York nearby, and Portland, the largest city in the state, within reach as well. Limited gay nightlife provides some evening activity, although many visitors opt for a quiet night with their traveling companions.

Accommodations

In-season is generally late spring until the end of summer; off-season is the rest of the year.

Gazebo   592 Main Street (Route 1); 207-646-3733; www.gaze boguesthouse.com (gay/straight, 9 rooms, $109–$170/$65–$140, closed Jan.). This Greek Revival farmhouse features rooms with air-conditioning, some of which have private baths. Full complimentary continental breakfasts, and there's a pool for warm-weather visitors. The beach is within walking distance.

Inn at Two Village Square   135 Route 1; 207-646-5779 (mostly men, 18 rooms, call for rates). This property features a hot tub, pool, sun deck, common kitchen, and TV lounge. Rooms have full amenities.

Rockmere Lodge   150 Stearns Rd.; 207-646-2985; www.rock mere.com (gay/straight, 8 rooms, $125–$190/$100–$130). Rooms all include private bath, cable TV, and paddle fans, plus basic amenities. Continental breakfast served with room rate.

Yellow Monkey   168 Main St.; 207-646-9056 (men and women; 40 rooms, call for rates). This property features an exercise room, Jacuzzi, and sun deck. Rates vary by room type, which range from those with a shared bathroom to self-sufficient units.

For More Information

Ogunquit Chamber of Commerce, 207-646-5533; www.ogun quit.org This mainstream organization can provide general information about tourism, accommodations, and attractions in the region.

Russian River, California

"Russian River is the perfect antidote when you want to get away from the fast urban pace of San Francisco or Los Angeles, but you still want to feel comfortable," says Victor Lopez, a southern Californian who enjoys the long drive north to this quiet, gay-popular region located about an hour and a half from San Francisco.

"Plus, it's mixed," adds his friend, Tanya Hilton. "The gay men outnumber the lesbians, as usual, but there are enough lesbians to make us feel comfortable, too."

Russian River is one of those places where lesbians and gay men go to relax. There's not much high-speed activity to get you pumped up. Instead, this progressive-minded region, dominated by the town of Guerneville, is home to pleasant, reasonably priced bed and breakfasts and easygoing activities. Damage from two major floods thankfully has been dealt with, leaving a charming community.

"I've come up here with friends just to hang out," says Victor. "We tour the region, hitting some of the wineries, then maybe go out for a good meal and just chill. It's no Palm Springs, and I'm glad about that."

THE KIND OF VACATION YOU CAN EXPECT HERE   This is not a party town, rather a place to enjoy the pleasures of small-town living, minus the usual closed-mindedness. Small stores and reasonable restaurants offer some activity, while a limited disco/bar scene keeps people moving at night. The wineries of the Napa and Sonoma valleys are a short drive away.

Accommodations

Russian River's in-season is generally from spring through the beginning of fall.

Fifes   16467 River Rd., Guerneville; 707-869-0656; www.fifes. com (gay/lesbian, 50 cabins, campsites, $50–$250/$50–$100). Cabins have one or two rooms, and there is also a two-bedroom cottage available. All include full amenities plus wet bar. The

---

TRAVEL TIP

Financial Services   There aren't too many instances where financial service companies have tailored their products for gay and lesbian travelers. American Express hasn't exactly done that either, but they've come mighty close with their travelers' checks.

You may have seen the ads in gay publications for their "Cheques for Two" program. The travelers' checks function like any other, with the additional convenience that they carry two signatures and can be used by two people. In the mainstream ads, this means a husband and wife. Their gay-specific ads display the signatures of same-sex couples on the checks, giving gay travelers the green light to use them during their romantic holidays abroad.

For information, call your local bank or American Express at 800-528-4800.

---

property features a restaurant, pool table, private beach, pool, sun deck, gym. Fifteen acres of gay fun.

Highlands Resort   14000 Woodland Dr., Guerneville; 707-869-0333 (gay/lesbian, 16 rooms and cabins, $45–$130/$40–$100, camping $20–$25 per person). Amenities vary here, where cabins feature kitchens. Guests can go nude at the pool and hot tub.

Retreat Resort and Spa   14711 Armstrong Woods Rd., Guerneville; www.retreatresort.com 707-869-2706 (gay/lesbian, 15 rooms, call for rates). Amenities vary at this guest house. Includes outdoor pool, Jacuzzi, and full spa.

Schoolhouse Canyon Park   12600 River Road, Guerneville, CA 95446; 707-869-2311 (mostly gay and lesbian, camping, call for rates). This property offers the camping experience, plus a private beach.

Willows   15905 River Rd., Guerneville; 707-869-2824; www.willowsrussianriver.com (gay/lesbian, 13 rooms, $79–$139/$69–$129). Located on five acres, this guest house offers full amenities plus VCR and ceiling fan. Continental breakfast is served, and the property features a hot tub, sauna, common kitchen, and video library, as well as a sun deck, private beach, and a dock on the Russian River. Canoes and kayaks available in the summer months.

For More Information

Gay Russian River, www.gayrussianriver.com

Russian River Gay and Lesbian Business Association, 707-869-GLBA

Russian River Chamber of Commerce and Visitors Center, 877-644-9001 or 707-869-9000, www.russianriver.com

10

SPECIAL EVENTS

"I met a lot of people in Europe. I even encountered myself."

—James Baldwin

We homosexuals are famous for our special events. After all, what would June be without Dykes on Bykes or men dressed as nuns?

Whether it's local celebrations that light up your hometown, or massive events that make you travel across the continent, these gatherings are something we look forward to every year.

It's absolutely impossible to catalog all the many special events that take place across the country each year—they vary so widely in terms of size, purpose, and popularity that it's futile to even try. Instead, these listings include some of the larger pride celebrations, events, film festivals, and parties. Exact dates and locations vary from year to year, but in most cases the months and the cities remain constant. You can call the information numbers to verify—and remember that you can attend many of these events as part of a package deal from various tour operators. Talk to your friendly travel agent to find out the details.

January

Aspen & Lesbian Gay Ski Week, Aspen, CO; 800-367-8290, www.gayskiweek.com. A whole week of benefits, parties, concerts, comedy nights, auctions, giveaways, fashion shows—and, oh yeah, skiing.

Blue Ball, Philadelphia, PA; 215-575-1110, www.blueball philly.com. A weekend of AIDS benefits.

Midsumma Festival, Melbourne, Australia; www.midsumma. org.au, 03-534-0781. Arts and a cultural festival rule this annual gay and lesbian event. Runs for three weeks.

February

Carnival in Rio, Rio de Janeiro, Brazil. Klamba, Above & Beyond Tours (see Glossary) and other companies offers package tours. Lots of fun for men and women.

HERO, Auckland, New Zealand; 9-307-1057; www.hero.org.nz. Fax 9-307-6824. Two weeks of fund-raising, parties, and cultural events mark New Zealand's largest gay event.

Mardi Gras, New Orleans, LA; www.mardigras.com (falls somewhere between February 3 and March 9). It's gay, it's lesbian, it's straight. It's Mardi Gras, an experience unlike any other. Call the Lesbian and Gay Community Center of New Orleans for the gay angle: 504-945-1103, http://gccno.org.

Saint-at-Large White Party, New York City, NY; 212-674-8541; www.saintatlarge.com. A major circuit event that recalls the glory days of the Saint, one of New York's premier gay discos. Held in a different location each year (the club itself no longer exists), it's a fund-raiser and an excuse to party—decked out all in white, of course—at the same time.

Gay & Lesbian Ski Week at Whistler Resort, Out on the Slopes Productions, 888-ALTITUDE or 604-688-5079; www.out

ontheslopes.com. This annual event brings thousands of gay and lesbian ski enthusiasts to the slopes of British Columbia, Canada.

Winter Gayla, Fort Lauderdale, FL; 954-525-4567; www.gay lauderdale.com/calendar.htm. This weekend celebration features a beach party, pride festival and parade, and a tour aboard a ship aptly named the Jungle Queen.

March

Dinah Shore Golf Week, Palm Springs, CA; 310-281-1715; www.9-web.com/gay-travel/21_dinah.htm. A popular event for lesbian golf enthusiasts, their friends, and a rising number of lesbians who don't even care about golf. Plenty of celebration to accompany the competition.

Sydney Gay and Lesbian Mardi Gras, Sydney, Australia; 011-61-2-9557-4332. Men and women from across the globe converge on Sydney for a month of parties and events. Feb 8–March 2, 2002.

Saint-at-Large Black Party, New York City, NY; 212-674-8541; www.saintatlarge.com/blackpty.html. Remember the Saint-at-Large White Party in February? This is the same idea, only you wear black.

Gay Ski Week, Lenzerheide, Switzerland; 011-41-1-725-4441. Men and women. www.cginternational.fsnet.co.uk/sking.htm

White Party, Palm Springs, CA; 310-659-6666. An Easter weekend of partying and entertainment; mostly men.

Winter Party, Miami Beach, FL; 800-494-8487; www.winter party.com. A beach party and AIDS benefit.

April

BeachFest, Daytona Beach, FL; 904-322-8003. Gay spring break celebration.

Cherry Jubilee, Washington, DC; 800-519-7792; www.cherry fund.com. A weekend of parties to benefit several non-profit groups.

Lesbian Dude Ranch Weekend, Poconos area, Pennsylvania; 610-268-3572. Women who yearn for the life of a cowgirl (or who simply enjoy being outdoors) are bound to like this weekend of old-fashioned dude ranch fun.

Queen's Day and Tulip Festival, Amsterdam, the Netherlands. Call Amsterdam's gay information center at 011-31-20-623-40-79 or the Netherlands Board of Tourism in the U.S. at 212-370-7360. This mainstream event is also one of the biggest gay gatherings in the Netherlands.

May

California AIDS Ride, San Francisco to Los Angeles, CA; 800-474-3395. A benefit bike ride.

Gay Pride March, Palm Springs, CA; 619-324-0178. Memorial Day weekend, when Gay Pride takes to the streets of this resort town, with plenty of parties and events all weekend.

Motor Ball, Detroit, MI; 810-358-9849, www.geared4life.org. Detroit's biggest gay and lesbian dance party.

International Mr. Leather Contest, Chicago, IL; 800-545-6735. Every Memorial Day weekend, hundreds of leather enthusiasts gather to choose the man who will represent them for the year. Lots of leather-themed parties and events.

Pridefest, Philadelphia, PA; 215-732-FEST, www.pridefest.org. A week-long celebration of all things gay and lesbian.

Razzle Dazzle Dallas, Dallas, TX; 214-528-4233; 214-407-3553. Gay festival.

Splash Days, Austin, TX; 512-476-3611. Parties, a beer barge, and the clothing is sometimes optional!

Sydney Leather Pride Week, Sydney, Australia, 011-52-61-2-9331-8608; www.sydneyleatherpride.org. Leather festivities down under.

June

June is historically lesbian and gay pride month, and just about every major city in the country—plus some cities abroad—

have something planned. Following are some of the contact numbers for more information; note that the International Association of Lesbian, Gay, Bisexual, Transgendered Pride Coordinators maintains a listing of pride dates on the Internet. Visit them on the World Wide Web at http://www.interpride.org.

Atlanta, GA: 770-662-4533
Chicago, IL: Pride Chicago, 312-348-8243
Columbus, OH: 614-299-7764
Denver, CO: 303-831-6268
Fort Lauderdale, FL: 305-771-1653
Houston, TX: 713-529-6979
Kansas City, MO: 816-561-9717
Los Angeles, CA: 213-860-0701
Minneapolis, MN: 612-377-8141
New York City, NY: 212-80-PRIDE
Pittsburgh, PA: 412-422-3060
Portland, OR: 503-295-9788
St. Louis, MO: 314-772-8888
Salt Lake City, UT: 801-539-8800
San Diego, CA: 619-29-PROUD
San Francisco, CA: 415-864-3733
Santa Barbara, CA: 805-963-3636
Seattle, WA: 206-292-1035
Toronto, Ontario, Canada: 416-92-PRIDE
Washington, DC: 202-986-1119

Other June events

Gay Day at Disney World, near Orlando, FL.; 407-843-4297, www.gayday.com. See Chapter Five for more details.

Key West Gay Arts Festival, Key West, FL; 800-429-9759. Artwork, artisans, and art lovers from across the country and abroad converge on Key West for several days of exhibits and events.

Queen's Birthday Ball, Sydney, Australia. Call Gay and Lesbian WotsOn, an information line, in Sydney at 011-61-2-361-0655, or the Gay and Lesbian Line at 011-61-2-360-2211, or the

Australian Tourist Commission at 800-445-4400. Still more partying for lesbians and gay men in Australia.
Russian River Rodeo, Russian River, CA; 707-869-GLBA. A
rodeo and related events. (For more details, see Chapter Eight.)
San Francisco International Lesbian and Gay Film Festival,
San Francisco, CA; 415-703-8650, www.frameline.org. Films from
around the world.

July

Bastille Day, Paris, France. Call the French Government
Tourist Office at 212-757-1125. Several tour operators can
arrange for you to celebrate this traditional French holiday in
typical gay style.
Halstead Market Days, Chicago, IL; 312-883-0500; www.
northalsted.com. A neighborhood street festival that takes
place in July or August.
Mr. Queensland Competition, Brisbane, Australia. Call Gay-
line at 011-61-7-3839-3277, or the Australian Tourist Commission
at 800-445-4400. Who is the fairest one of all?
Outfest, Los Angeles, CA; 213-951-1247; www.outfest.org. A
lesbian and gay film and video festival.

August

Gay Pride, Montreal, Quebec, Canada. 514-285-4011; www.
diverscite.org
Gay Pride, Orange County, CA; 714-637-7768. Various local
and regional organizations, along with thousands of other lesbians and gay men from the area, come together to show their
pride with a parade, special events, and parties.
Hotlanta, Atlanta, GA; 404-874-3976; www.hotlanta.org. River
expo, floating-down-the-river party, Mr. & Miss Hotlanta contest,
plenty of other parties.
Provincetown Carnival, Provincetown, MA; 800-637-8696;
www.ptown.org. Parties and celebrations.

Womyn's Music Festival, Hart, MI; 231-757-4766; www.mich fest.com. Musicians and lesbians from across the country and abroad gather for a few days of song and celebration.

September

Folsom Street Fair, San Francisco, CA; 415-861-3247; www.fol somstreetfair.com. Vendors, fun, and leather out on the street.

Gay Oktoberfest, Munich, Germany. Sure, it's not quite October, but gay people are always ahead of their time.

Key West Theatre Festival, Key West, FL; 305-294-4603, www.keywesttheatrefestival.org. Local and visiting writers and performers show off their stuff, with specially priced tickets available to performances.

Labor Day LA, Los Angeles, CA; 800-429-8747/800-522-7329. Four days of parties at various locations; a fund-raiser for Foundation for Educational Research, for AIDS education, direct service, and research organizations.

Mr. Drummer Contest, San Francisco, CA; 415-252-1195. Which man looks best in leather? You'll find out here.

Red Party, Columbus, OH; 614-294-8309. Days of partying, circuit-style, in the heartland.

Southern Decadence, New Orleans, LA; 504-529-2860, www.southerndecadence.net. Who says you have to wait for Mardi Gras to have fun?

Texas Freedom Day Parade, Dallas, TX; 214-538-4233. Celebrates the repealing of the state's sodomy law.

Womenfest, Key West, FL; 800-535-7797, www.womenfest.net. A week's worth of parties and events for women, including comedy nights, a lesbian film festival, street fair, parties, and cruises.

October

Black & Blue Weekend, Montreal, Quebec, Canada; 514-875-7026. Several days of partying, mostly for gay men.

Castro Street Fair, San Francisco, CA; 415-467-3354, www. castrostreetfair.org. The classic gay and lesbian street fair.

Halloween Parade, New York City, NY; 212-475-3333, www.halloween-nyc.com. Thousands of gay and straight people take to the streets of Greenwich Village, in full costume.

Key West Fantasyfest, Key West, FL; 305-296-1817, www. fantasyfest.net. Celebrating Halloween gaily with outrageous costumes and parties.

New Orleans Gay Pride, New Orleans, LA; 504-457-7657, www.neworleansgaypride.com. Gay and lesbian pride festival.

Ohio Lesbian Festival, Columbus, OH; 614-267-3953, www. ohiolba.org. Parties, music, and political and social events mark this annual celebration.

Sleaze Ball, Sydney, Australia; 011-61-3-852-2757, www.sleaze ball.com.au. If you're willing to travel a long way for a circuit party, this is where to go—ask thousands of men who've made the trip.

Women's Week, Provincetown, MA; www.womeninnkeep ers.com. Parties and events for women fill the streets of P-town.

November

AIDS Dance-a-thon, New York City, NY; 212-807-9255, www.gmhc.org. Massive benefit for Gay Men's Health Crisis.

Gay Day at Disneyland, Anaheim, CA; 714-778-600, www. gayday2.com. A weekend at Disneyland.

Gay Rodeo, Palm Springs, CA; 760-318-7702, www.igra.com. One of your last chances to join the gay rodeo circuit before the end of the year. (See chapter eight for more details.)

The White Party, Miami, FL; 305-667-9296, www.whiteparty. net. A beautifully restored mansion is the setting for this AIDS benefit.

Winter Party, Miami Beach, FL; 305-460-3115; www. winterparty.com. One of the major gay fund-raising parties in the Miami area, with dancing and entertainment of various forms all night.

DIRECTORY OF GAY, LESBIAN, AND GAY-FRIENDLY TRAVEL RESOURCES

Following is a listing of all the gay-friendly companies and businesses mentioned in this book, along with a brief description of the company and the products and services it offers.

Above & Beyond Tours 230 N. Via Las Palmas, Palm Spring, CA 92262; 800-397-2681 or 760-325-0702. Fax 760-325-1702. Website: www.abovebeyondtours.com. Group and independent tour packages to Europe, Latin America, Pacific region. Active vacations, dive tours, South Pacific excursions including Australia and the Sydney Gay & Lesbian Mardi Gras, Carnival in Rio, Thanksgiving and Queen's Day in Amsterdam, Paris, Italy. Packages are sold only through travel agents.

Adventure Bound Expeditions 711 Walnut St., Boulder, CO 80302; 303-449-0990. Fax 303-449-9038. Website: www.adventure boundmen.com. Escorted tours focusing on outdoor activities across the globe.

All About Destinations 3819 North Third St., Phoenix, AZ 85012; 800-375-2703. E-mail: proudmembr@aol.com. Gay and lesbian group cruises to Alaska, Acapulco, other destinations aboard mainstream ships. Escorted tour packages, usually involving special events such as Carnival in Venice, Italy, and the Bolshoi Theater in Moscow.

Alyson Adventures P.O. Box 181223, Boston, MA 02118; 800-825-9766 or 617-247-8170. Fax 617-542-9189. Website: www. alysonadventures.com. Active vacations, cycling, hiking, skiing, mountaineering in Europe and the United States, Sydney Gay &

Lesbian Mardi Gras, diving in the Caribbean. Gay singles trips also offered.

Atlantis Events   9060 Santa Monica Blvd., Suite 310, West Hollywood, CA 90069; 800-628-5268 or 310-281-5450. Fax 310-281-5455. Website: www.atlantisevents.com. All-inclusive vacation packages at Club Med properties in the Caribbean and Bahamas, Windstar cruises to the South Pacific and other destinations; trips to Sydney Gay & Lesbian Mardi Gras includes a visit to an all-inclusive private island resort. Website: http://www.province town.com/village/women/clublebon/clublebon.html. Women-only trips to Mexico and the Caribbean (e.g., Barbados); gay and lesbian family vacations (including the kids) to Mexico's Yucatan peninsula.

Club RSVP   See RSVP Travel Productions.

Club Travel   8739 Santa Monica Blvd., West Hollywood, CA 90069; 800-429-8747 or 310-358-2200. Fax 310-353-2222. South Pacific excursions, including Fiji and the Sydney Gay & Lesbian Mardi Gras, featuring full-service apartment accommodations with kitchen, laundry facilities, CD stereo systems, gym, Jacuzzi, pool.

Community Marketing   584 Castro St, San Francisco, CA 94114; 415-437-3800. Fax 415-552-5104. Website: www.mark8ing. com. A company that helps travel businesses market themselves to the lesbian and gay community, Community Marketing also hosts gay travel expos throughout the United States at different times during the year. The company also publishes *The Specialist,* a monthly newsletter for travel professionals, and runs Gayjet.com and the Travel Alternatives Group.

Connections Tours   169 Lincoln Rd., Suite 302, Miami Beach, FL 33139; 800-OUT-TIME or 305-673-3153. Fax 305-673-6501. E-mail: connectfl@aol.com. Packaged trips to various destinations in Florida, including Miami Beach, Orlando, Key West, Fort Lauderdale, Tampa.

David Tours   310 Dahlia Place, Suite A, Corona del Mar, CA 92675-2821; 888-723-0699. Fax 714-723-0666. Website: www.david tours.com. Escorted tours to Hungary, Czech Republic, Vienna,

Paris, New Orleans, and South Africa. Trips to each destination include social gatherings with local friends.

Doin' It Right Travel 800-936-DOIN or 619-297-3642, www.doinitright.com. Gay and lesbian tour packages to Puerto Vallarta, Mexico. The company provides information about gay nightlife, gay beaches, gay-friendly restaurants, etc.

Earth Walks P.O. Box 8534, Santa Fe, NM 87501; 505-988-4157. Active vacations, visits to Native American ruins in New Mexico.

Eurway Tour & Cruise Club 26 Sixth St., Stamford, CT 06905; 800-550-0091. Eurway offers escorted and independent travel to Greece, Turkey, and Egypt, both by land (with villa accommodations) and sea (by yacht).

Florida Adventures P.O. Box 677923, Orlando, FL 32867; 407-677-0655. Fax 407-677-0238. Luxury adventure cruises in the Caribbean, leaving from South Florida.

Good Time Tours 450 W. 62nd St., Miami Beach, FL 33140; 888-GAYFLAS or 305-864-9431. Fax 305-866-6955. E-mail: GAYFLA@aol.com; Website: http://www.gayday.com. The official tour operator for Gay Day at Disney, this company's hotel packages are available through travel agents.

Hanns Ebensten Travel 513 Fleming St., Key West, FL 33040; 305-294-8174. Fax 305-292-9665. Website: www.wetravel.com. A wide variety of escorted gay tours focusing on archeology, culture, wildlife, nature, history. Destinations include South America, Europe, Africa, and Asia.

Hawk, I'm Your Sister P.O. Box 9109, Santa Fe, NM 87504; 505-984-2268. Fax 909-498-7793. Website: www.womansplace.com. Women-only active vacations, featuring retreats, wilderness and canoe trips. Destinations include Norway, Russia, Peru, New Zealand and the U.S.

Her Wild Song P.O. Box 515, Brunswick, ME 04011; 207-721-9005. Fax 207-721-0235. Active vacations, women-only kayaking, canoeing, and backpacking tours. Most trips have a spiritual focus, and destinations include New England, Florida, Nova Scotia, and the western U.S.

Himalayan High Treks   241 Dolores St., San Francisco, CA 94103-2211; 800-455-8735 or 415-861-2391. E-mail: effie@well.com. Gay escorted tours of Nepal, India, Tibet, and Bhutan.

International Gay and Lesbian Travel Association   P.O. Box 4974, Key West, FL 33041-4974; 800-448-8550 or 305-292-0217. Fax 305-296-6633, www.iglta.org. An association of travel professionals, tour operators, and suppliers who serve lesbian and gay travelers. The IGTA serves as a networking source and a clearinghouse for information, and can provide information and referrals for travel agents and tour operators.

Journeys by Sea   1402 E. Las Olas Blvd., Suite 122, Fort Lauderdale, FL 33301; 800-825-3681. Fax 800-825-5956. Gay yacht vacations across the globe, with the option of booking the whole yacht or joining an existing excursion with your own stateroom.

Lizard Head Expeditions   1280 Humboldt St., #32, Denver, CO 80218; 888-540-2737 or 303-831-7090. Fax 303-831-7090. E-mail: info@lizardhead.com; Website: http://lizardhead.com. Active vacations for men and women in the American West: hiking, skiing, canyon and mountain tours, with departures from Crested Butte, Telluride, and Moab. Lizard Head's guides offer instruction in a range of "wilderness skills," although accommodations are in deluxe properties.

Mariah Wilderness Expeditions   P.O. Box 248, Port Richmond, CA 94807; 800-462-7424 or 510-233-2303. Fax 510-233-0956. Active vacations, most of which are for women only, including whitewater rafting, sailing excursions. Destinations include the western United States, Europe, South and Central America, and Australia.

Men on Vacation   1040 University Ave. Ste. B201, San Diego, CA 92103; 888-333-4668 or 619-682-5105. Fax 619-682-1504. Website: www.menonvacation.com. Active vacations, ski vacations, tall ship cruises South Pacific tours to destinations like New Zealand, Hawaii, and Australia, including Sydney Gay and Lesbian Mardi Gras and packages to the Man Friday Resort in Fiji. Men on Vacation has teamed up with Certified Vacations, a mainstream tour operator, to offer air-inclusive packages to several domestic and international gay-friendly destinations.

Mi Casa Su Casa PO Box 4714, Walnut Creek, CA 94596; Website: www.gayhometrade.com. Lesbian, gay, and gay-friendly home exchanges in the U.S. and abroad. While you stay in a member's home, they stay in yours.

Mountain Madness 4218 SW Alaska St., #206 Seattle, WA 98116; 206-937-8389. Website: www.mountainmadness.com Mountain-climbing trips to the Pacific Northwest, Africa, Nepal, and other destinations.

New England Vacation Tours P.O. Box 571, Route 100, West Dover, VT 05356; 800-742-7669 or 802-464-2076. Fax 802-464-2629. Mainstream tour operator that offers some all-gay tours and gay-sensitive mainstream tours. Themes include fall foliage and party weekends.

Ocean Voyager Cruise Consultants 1717 N. Bayshore Dr., #3246, Miami, FL 33132-1167; 800-435-2531. Website: www.ocean voyager.com. Gay group travel with mainstream cruise companies, including Princess Cruises, Holland America Line, Majesty, Celebrity, and Royal Caribbean. Itineraries cover the Caribbean, New England, Florida, Europe and transatlantic, and Alaska.

Odyssey Adventures P.O. Box 923094, Filmar, CA 91392; 805-222-7788. Fax 805-222-7787. Website: www.odysseyadven tures.com. This company sells tickets for gay and lesbian night at Disneyland.

Olivia Cruises and Resorts 4400 Market St., Oakland, CA 94608; 800-631-6277 or 510-655-0364; Fax 510-655-4334. Website: www.olivia.com. A wide variety of women-only cruise and resort packages, including ski resorts and Club Med properties in Ixtapa and Sonora, Mexico. Cruise destinations include Alaska, the French/Italian Riviera, the Caribbean, the Mediterranean, and Tahiti.

Out on the Slopes Productions 1238 Melville St., Suite 204, Vancouver, BC V6E 4N2, Canada; 888-ALTITUDE or 604-688-5079. Fax 604-688-5033. Makes arrangements for Gay & Lesbian Ski Week at Whistler Resort, held every February.

Outwest Global Adventures P.O. Box 8451, Missoula, MT 59807; 800-743-0458 or 406-446-1533. Fax 406-446-1338. Website: www.outwestadventures.com. Active vacations, rafting, backpacking, hiking, rail riding, horseback riding, mountain biking, skiing, snowboarding; focus is on the American West and abroad.

Pied Piper Travel   330 W. 42nd St., Suite 1804, New York, NY 10036; 800-TRIP-312 or 212-239-2412. Fax 212-239-2275. Website: www.gaygroupcruises.com. A travel agency that caters to gay and lesbian travelers, specializing in gay group cruises aboard the *QE2,* with itineraries that include Hawaii, the Caribbean, New England/Canada, the Panama Canal, Bermuda, Europe, and, of course, the traditional transatlantic crossing.

Port Yacht Charters   9 Belleview, Port Washington, NY 11050; 800-213-0465. Website: www.portyachtcharters.com. Private yacht charters in the Caribbean, New England, and the Mediterranean.

Progressive Travels   224 West Galer, Suite C, Seattle, WA 98119; 800-245-2229 or 206-285-1987. Fax 206-285-1988. A mainstream operator that offers gay bicycle and walking tours in France, Italy, and the United States.

Rainbow Country Tours   P.O. Box 333, Escalante, UT 84726; 800-826-4567. Guided trips on foot and by Jeep, in southern Utah.

Robin Tyler Tours   15842 Chase St., North Hills, CA 91343; 818-893-4075. Website: www.robintylertours.com. Women-only escorted tours worldwide, destinations vary yearly.

Royal Hawaiian Weddings   P.O. Box 424, Puunene, HI 96784; 800-659-1866. Website: www.royalhawaiianweddings.com. Weddings and commitment ceremonies for gay and lesbian couples, set in the Hawaiian islands.

RSVP Travel Productions   2535 25th Ave S, Minneapolis, MN 55406-1234; 800-328-RSVP. Website: www.rsvp.net. This company offers several travel products. RSVP Cruises offers all-gay cruise itineraries throughout Europe, South America, the Mediterranean, and the Caribbean, including a visit to New Orleans for Mardi Gras. Club RSVP offers all-gay, all-inclusive resort vacations, primarily in Mexico.

Sailing Affairs   404 E. 11th St., New York, NY 10009; 212-228-5755. This company offers group charters and trips for individuals aboard a thirty-eight-foot sailboat, with cabins to sleep a total of six people. Itineraries vary by request, and generally cover the entire East Coast.

Skylink Women's Travel 2953 Lincoln Blvd., Santa Monica, CA 90405; 800-CALL-SKY or 310-452-0506. Fax 310-452-0562. Website: www.skylinktravel.com. Women-only cruises, with itineraries including the United States, Europe, Hawaii, and Africa.

Spirit Journeys P.O. Box 5307, Santa Fe, NM 87502; 505-351-4004. Fax 505-351-4999. Website: www.spiritjourneys.com. Spiritual retreats in the United States, Mexico, and the Caribbean.

Tall Ship Adventures 1389 S. Havana St., Aurora, CO 80012; 800-662-0090 or 303-755-7983. Website: www.tallshipadventures.com. Gay-friendly cruises in the Caribbean.

Toto Tours 1326 West Albion Ave., Chicago, IL 60626-4753; 800-565-1241 or 773-274-8686. Fax 773-274-8695. Website: www.tototours.com. Active/adventure vacations. Activities include bicycling, horseback riding, whitewater rafting, hiking, kayaking, sailing, and photo safaris. Destinations include the Caribbean, Hawaii, Costa Rica, Mexico, Scotland, Utah, Tanzania, Alaska, the Grand Canyon, Yellowstone, the Netherlands, and the Pacific Northwest. Levels of activity, type of accommodation, and features included in the basic price vary by trip.

Travel Keys Tours P.O. Box 162266, Sacramento, CA 95816; 916-452-5200. Fax 916-452-5200. Men-only dungeon tours of Europe, focusing particularly on Germany; antiquing tours of England and France that are open to everyone, gay and straight alike.

Undersea Expeditions 4950 Lamont St., San Diego, CA 92109; 800-669-0310 or 858-270-2900. Fax 858-490-1002. Website: www.underseax.com. Escorted scuba vacations for beginners and experts to the South Pacific, Mexico, and Central America.

Water Fantaseas 122 Nurmi Dr., Fort Lauderdale, FL 33301; 954-524-1234. Website: www.waterfantaseas.com This company offers a forty-four-foot private yacht for charters from Fort Lauderdale, Florida.

Way to Go Costa Rica P.O. Box 31288, Raleigh, NC 27622-1288; 800-835-1223. Fax 919-787-1952. Website: www.waytogocostarica.com. Wholesale travel agency that owns Destination

Costa Rica, a ground operator in San Jose, Costa Rica. Specializes in mainstream and gay-specific trips to Costa Rica, with varied activities such as snorkeling, canoeing, horseback riding, hiking, canal cruising, fishing, and golfing.

Wild Hearts Adventures c/o International Tours, RR2 Box 443B Lake Rd., Avondale, PA 19311; 610-925-3922. Active vacations, women-only excursions, including Caribbean cruises, visits to dude ranches, trips to Europe.

Windjammer Barefoot Cruises 8235 Santa Monica Blvd., Suite 214, West Hollywood, CA 90046; 800-2-GAY-CRUISE or 213-654-7700. Fax 213-654-7909. Website: www.gaywindjammer.com. Caribbean windjammer cruises.

Womantours P.O. Box 931, Driggs, ID 83422; 800-247-1444. Bicycling tours in the United States, including the national parks of Utah.

Women Sail Alaska P.O. Box 20348, Juneau, AK 99802; 888-272-4525, www.alaska.net/~sailak/. Sailings for women only in southeast Alaska on a thirty-foot sloop, offering whale watching, photography, beach walking, birding, and fishing. Also, the opportunity to learn sailing skills and boat handling.

INDEX

ABOUT THE AUTHOR

Mark Chesnut's addiction to travel has colored his entire life. Always seeking to get the most mileage out of everything, he engineered his professional and personal life to revolve around frequent flyer mileage and boarding passes.

Mark works full-time as a senior editor at *Travel Weekly,* the national newspaper of the travel industry. From 1993 to 1998, he was also editor-in-chief of *Skyjack Magazine,* a quarterly publication he founded for gay people who fly. Under the *Skyjack* banner, Mark organized "Turbulence," a series of successful airline-themed fundraisers—complete with drag-queen flight attendants and go-go boy baggage handlers—to raise funds for airline employees with AIDS, HIV, and other life-threatening illnesses.

In addition to *Travel Weekly* and *Skyjack Magazine,* Mark's writing has appeared in *The Advocate,* the *Boston Herald, Business Traveler International, Emerge, Genre, Instinct, Interval World, Latin Trade, New York Press, Out & About, PlanetOut, TravelAge,* and *Travel Management Daily.* He was a contributing author to *Uncommon Heroes* (Fletcher Press, 1994) and *We Are Everywhere: A Historical Sourcebook in Gay and Lesbian Politics* (Routledge, 1995/1997). His travel photography has been published in *Instinct, TravelAge,* and *Travel Weekly,* and his collection of travel photography—and some choice pieces of his writing—can be seen at www.markchesnut.com.

Mark has led workshops and seminars on gay travel, travel marketing, and travel writing for *Travel Weekly, TravelAge Magazine,* the National Lesbian and Gay Journalists Association, and the International Conference on Lesbian and Gay Tourism.

A specialist in Latin America, Mark received a 2001 *Premio Vallarta* award from the Puerto Vallarta Tourism Board, for journalistic excellence in covering that Mexican destination.

He has been quoted in *Air Transport World* and interviewed on PBS, WIVB-TV Buffalo, and CNN Headline News (albeit for about four seconds because he happened to be standing in line at the Eastern Air Shuttle). His ridiculously large collection of airline memorabilia has been featured in *Frequent Flyer*, Condé Nast's *Lucky Magazine,* and *Time Out New York.*

Mark has flown more than fifty different airlines to more than forty nations in the Americas, Europe, Africa, and Asia—from Bangkok to Buenos Aires, from Paducah to Prague. He is originally from Brockport, a small town in western New York State, although he is quick to acknowledge that frequent visits to his extended family in Kentucky were key to his developing a life-long travel bug. Since 1986, he has called the New York City area his home—where he lives with his partner in love and travel, Angel Pabón Ramírez. Mark prefers an aisle seat, non-smoking, with the chicken entrée. You can send him your best travel tales at ChesnutAir@aol.com or www.markchesnut.com.